Regulation and Expansion of Health Facilities

Eleanore Rothenberg

The Praeger Special Studies program—utilizing the most modern and efficient book production techniques and a selective worldwide distribution network—makes available to the academic, government, and business communities significant, timely research in U.S. and international economic, social, and political development.

Regulation and Expansion of Health Facilities

The Certificate of Need Experience in New York State

PRAEGER SPECIAL STUDIES IN U.S. ECONOMIC, SOCIAL, AND POLITICAL ISSUES

Praeger Publishers   New York   Washington   London

Library of Congress Cataloging in Publication Data

Rothenberg, Eleanore.
     Regulation and expansion of health facilities.

     (Praeger special studies in U.S. economic, social,
and political issues)
     Bibliography: p.
     Includes index.
     1. Health facilities—Planning—New York (State)
2. Health facilities—New York (State)—Design and
construction.   3. Health facilities—Law and legislation—
New York (State) I. Title.
RA981.N7R67   362.1'09747   76-7381
ISBN 0-275-23080-5

PRAEGER PUBLISHERS
111 Fourth Avenue, New York, N.Y. 10003, U.S.A.

Published in the United States of America in 1976
by Praeger Publishers, Inc.

Printed in the United States of America

The author is indebted to many individuals who gave freely of their time, energy, and special skills during the course of this study. Grateful acknowledgment is made first to Professor Charles Arnold, M.D., New York University Graduate School of Public Administration, the one individual who was most responsible for the study's successful completion, for his continuous commitment throughout and for helping me develop an understanding of the language, uses, and limitations of research methods in the social sciences; to Lowell E. Bellin, M.D., New York City Commissioner of Health, for his enthusiasm, invaluable direction, and wise counsel; the late Professor Howard Brown, M.D., New York University Graduate School of Public Administration and former New York City Commissioner of Hospitals, for sharing his extensive knowledge of the New York City health care system; Mr. Alan Bell, Lecturer, New York University Graduate School of Public Administration, for an introduction to statistics; Melvin Schwartz, M.D., Ph.D., Assistant Commissioner for Bio-Statistics, New York City Department of Health, for helping me translate a rudimentary understanding of the methods of quantitative analysis into a useful research tool, and for the hours of detailed analysis which improved, immeasurably, the quality of the presentation and interpretation of the findings; Mr. Irvin G. Wilmot, Executive Vice President and Mr. Peter Hughes, Assistant to the Executive Vice President, New York University Medical Center, for their endless cooperation and for enriching my insights into health planning; Mr. Daniel Zwick, Associate Administrator for Planning, Evaluation and Legislation, Department of Health, Education and Welfare, for his early encouragement and continuing support of the study; Jack Haldeman, M.D., Director, and Mr. Joseph Peter, former Associate Director, Health and Hospital Planning Council of Southern New York, Inc., for their extraordinary help in providing relevant information and opportunities for observation; Mr. Marvin Roth, Director, Health Affairs, Department of City Planning, and formerly of the Health and Hospital Planning Council, for advice on validation of the data used in the analyses; Mr. Leonard Schraeger, Mr. Howard Moses, Mr. Herbert Williams, Sigmund Friedman, M.D., and Ms. Dorothy Woodhead, of the Health and Hospital Planning Council, for sharing insights and information; Mr. Walter Wenkert, Mr. Anthony Mott, John Hill, Ph.D., Mr. Edward Lane, Ms. Gloria Haynie, and the Honorable Marion Folsom, for providing important background and historical information and for the opportunity to observe the Genesee Region Health Planning Council in action; Peter Rogatz, M.D., Senior Vice President, Blue Cross and Blue Shield of New York, for his keen interest and constructive criticism; William Leavy, M.D., New York State Department of

Health, for assistance in providing raw data for the analyses; Ms. Deborah Paul Rogers, for her articulate and perceptive comments; Ms. Jean-Marie Moore for her encouragement; Angelo Ferrara, M. D. , for his assistance at a critical point in the study.

Finally, I am grateful to my husband, Stanley, and to my three sons, David, Michael, and Seth, for their love and infinite patience.

CONTENTS

LIST OF TABLES AND MAP

Many believe that a national health care delivery system requires health and hospital planning and that such planning can only be effective, or can be more effective, where there exists a regulatory mechanism at the local, state, or federal level to prevent construction of new facilities and substantial changes in existing facilities, where such construction and changes are thought not to be in the public interest.

New York was the first state to enact certificate of need laws. [1] Many states have since used New York's legislative program as a guide for development of similar legislation, and recently enacted federal programs contain similar provisions. [2] Accordingly, the following question may be asked: On what evidence are these legislative decisions being based?

A review of the literature establishes that there has been little analysis of empirical evidence to either support or refute the proposition that the certificate of need legislation has had the desired effect on health and hospital planning processes or outcomes. This study is intended to provide such analysis.

The public interest in health and hospital planning apparent since the mid-1940s reached a new high in the last decade or so because of spiraling hospital costs in the face of a growing public demand for a more rational health care delivery system. Herbert Klarman attributes that interest to

> a large amount of social capital (from philanthropy and tax funds) invested in hospitals; the high cost of construction (attributable, in part, to the increased space required for supporting services) and the difficulty of financing it; and the rising unit cost of hospital care.[3]

Despite the activities in recent years of hospital planning agencies, overbuilding or duplication of costly facilities has been typical of some areas of the country, while other sections remain underserved. The maldistribution of facilities has been attributed, in part, to the absence (until recently and then in only several states) of regulatory authority to restrict unnecessary or undesirable projects.

New York, due to intense public pressure during the early 1960s, enacted the first such laws aimed at providing planning agencies at the state and local level with "clout." (Technically, the regional planning agencies are advisory. However, very often their recommendations are adopted by the commissioner, the Public Health Council, and the Hospital Review Council with respect to approval or disapproval of specific projects or applications in their jurisdictions.)

Under provisions of the Metcalf-McCloskey Act (Chapter 730, laws of 1964) and its 1965 amendments (Article 28), prior approval (certification of need) is required from the state commissioner of health in order to construct hospital and health-related facilities or to undertake substantial alterations, renovations, or modernization of facilities, or changes in services.

Thus, the concept of "voluntary" planning was replaced with a new approach to answering the health facility needs of the community involved, one which for the first time shifted the focus to regulation and control.

The objectives of this study are:

1. To describe recent trends in health and hospital planning which underlie the proposition that legal authority to regulate the planning process (certification of need) would help make it more effective than voluntary planning.

2. To document the events leading to passage of the certification of need legislation in New York State.

3. To evaluate the impact of the certificate of need legislation on health and hospital planning outcomes at the local (county) level.

This study is composed of four parts. Part I provides general background information on the evolution of regulatory programs affecting hospital facility construction. It is not a history of health facilities planning or of regulation of hospital construction, for these subjects are covered elsewhere in the literature, but some of the current trends and issues in health facility planning and regulation are identified. In the first chapter, changing concepts regarding the need for regulatory authority to make planning effective are examined (From Voluntarism to Regulation). The desirability or appropriateness of combining planning with a regulatory mechanism (The Planning-Regulation Dichotomy) is also considered. In Chapter 2, New York's regulatory mechanism is described. Included are some historical highlights, a brief summary of the major statutory provisions and selected amendments, and an overview of the review process and appeals procedures.

Part II is devoted to the research design. In Chapter 3, the assumptions underlying the legislation are explored and the questions which this study is attempting to answer are stated. Included is a review of selected works which focus on either areawide facility planning effectiveness or on particular certificate of need programs. The concept of evaluation is examined and the problem of selecting the proper framework is discussed. Chapter 4 is devoted to the research methodology and to the specification of study areas, the time period selected for study, and the outcomes (dependent variables) chosen to measure program impact. Other factors which might have influenced observed changes during the study period are also identified. Finally, limitations are stated and discussed.

In Part III the observed changes in general care and long-term care facilities before and after the introduction of the certificate of need program are presented and interpreted. In Chapter 5, a preliminary analysis is described. Significant differences among counties and planning regions are identified. Chapter 6 explains the analytical model used for evaluation of these observed changes, including the specification of the independent variables used in the model. The findings are presented in Chapters 7 and 8. Relationships between observed change in the number of beds in a particular study county and the county characteristics (as well as other independent variables) are shown through the use of simple and multiple correlations.

Part IV presents the study summary and conclusions. Chapter 9 is devoted to a recpitulation and discussion of the major findings as well as their implications. Suggestions are made for future research directions. In addition, a set of inferences which may be drawn, based on the findings of the study, are stated. The Epilogue describes the latest health planning legislation (Pub. L. 93-641) and the possible usefulness of the methods and findings of this study for others who may want to understand the complex problems associated with assessing the effect of certificate of need legislation programs.

NOTES

1. The Metcalf-McCloskey Act (Laws of 1964); New York State Public Health Law, Chapter 730; and Folsom Amendments (Laws of 1965), Chapter 795, Article 28, comprise the certificate of need authority in New York State.

2. Pub. L. 92-603, Section 1122, the Social Security Amendments of 1972, provides for denial of federal reimbursement on capital expenditures not approved by designated state and areawide facility planning units, and Pub. L. 93-641, enacted early in 1975, combines planning and regulation at the local and state levels.

3. Herbert Klarman: "Some Technical Problems in Areawide Planning for Hospital Care, " Journal of Chronic Diseases 17 (1964): 735.

1

HEALTH AND HOSPITAL
FACILITIES PLANNING
AND REGULATION

Although hospital and health facilities planning activities can be traced to the early 1920s and 1930s, it was during the period 1946 to 1966 that increasingly health planning had come to be regarded as a vehicle for rationalizing the health care system, for solving the health care "crisis," for moderating rapidly rising costs, especially hospital costs, and for assuring "the highest level of health attainable for every citizen."[1]

With only a few exceptions, the construction of an adequate number of facilities, especially in rural areas, was the major concern in most communities during the era following World War II. The Hill-Burton program, which was one of the first systematic attempts to help the states and local communities plan for and develop hospitals and health facilities and services, reflected these concerns and provided for matching funds to stimulate the building of new facilities.[2] For a number of reasons, little planning for hospital facilities existed prior to its enactment. During the Depression and until the end of the Second World War, there had been little or no construction of new facilities. Where hospitals were constructed, there were no guidelines to help determine where they would be located or which services they would provide.[3]

FROM VOLUNTARISM TO REGULATION

Before 1966 there was no official regulatory mechanism with respect to construction of new facilities or expansion of existing ones, nor was it then thought to be a necessary governmental function. Although there were a few health facility planning agencies at the time the Hill-Burton program was first enacted, they were voluntary. As an outgrowth of the voluntary health and welfare agencies which had sprung up during the 1920s and 1930s, these agencies were primarily concerned with fund raising, resource allocation, and effective delivery of needed social services.[4] After World War II, hospital capital fund requirements increased dramatically. As a result, the leaders of the voluntary health and welfare agencies perceived the need for an independent organization to handle the complex new problem of capital financing for hospitals and health facilities. According to Symond Gottlieb, the newly formed hospital planning agencies were "primarily interested in bricks and mortar developments" and especially in general care hospitals and in short-term beds.[5]

As they gained experience, health and hospital planning agencies changed their priorities and their methods. While the rising cost of hospital construction was still of great concern, a new emphasis was being placed on programs rather than solely on construction of physical facilities. Other issues emerged, including those relating to the manpower shortage, the rising costs of operating general hospitals, the need for alternatives to costly inpatient short-term hospital care, such as ambulatory and home care, and the need for special services for the chronically ill and mentally ill. There was a growing awareness of the problem of maldistribution of needed facilities and of the inability of voluntary planning agencies to regulate or influence the regulation of hospital construction. The size, location, or types of services to be provided in an area were a function of the sponsor's wishes or the local community's demands. Small (under 50 beds) institutions which were being established in close proximity to one another could not provide the best quality of care because each institution had to draw on a limited pool of highly trained personnel.[6]

There has been a great deal of discussion and acceptance over the years of the theoretical value of regionalization. In practice, however, the expansion of hospitals and health facilities has mostly remained a matter of private institutional decision-making and initiative.

In an attempt to effect change, Congress passed the Comprehensive Health Planning Act (1966) which created new requirements for consumer participation in decision-making processes affecting health care delivery systems.[7] New goals and requirements emerged as a result, and health planning at every level of government has been redirected.

Despite these shifts in focus, the emphasis on bricks and mortar and on hospital beds has never quite disappeared. Indeed, there is now a marked resurgence of interest in physical facilities planning. More important, the current debate about the issue of regulation and the need for certification of need mechanisms to restrict new construction not thought to be in the public interest has brought into sharp focus some of the underlying assumptions behind these regulatory programs.[8]

According to William Curran, the earliest "serious discussion of some form of public control over health-care facility growth" occurred during the 1959 meetings sponsored by the American Hospital Association (AHA) and the United States Public Health Service (USPHS). Curran states that these meetings were a result of the first denial by a state insurance commissioner of a requested Blue Cross rate increase. [9]

Joel J. May's history of the health planning movement describes these regional conferences at length.[10] However, he makes only brief mention of "the need for force or sanction to make planning work." May attributes these discussions to Ray Brown and John Zenger, the latter speaking for the AHA Council on Planning, Financing, and Prepayment. May suggested that the question of whether voluntary planning can be effective "in the absence of force (of law?) . . . to bring into being or to preserve an integrated system" remained unanswered. May's history was published in 1967.[11]

The work of the Joint AHA-USPHS Committee (1959-61) was summarized in a widely accepted report entitled Areawide Planning for Hospitals and Related Health Facilities.[12] The report became a basic guide for planning agencies and influenced federal support in the form of grants and operating funds for areawide planning agencies throughout the United States. The health planning movement was characterized by rapid growth during the early 1960s as reflected in the increased number of such agencies during that period.[13]

While health planning was gaining momentum in various parts of the country because of new federal programs directed at improving and extending health planning activities, events in New York State were taking a different turn. In 1964 and 1965 the first legislation establishing a regulatory mechanism to control hospital and health related facility expansion was enacted. The New York legislation which followed the state's studies of hospital costs and health insurance rates became the model for certificate of need laws in other states and at the federal level. (A more detailed description of the events in New York State leading to enactment of the certificate of need laws follows in Chapter 2.)

In 1968, the AHA officially adopted a position favoring the certification of need approach, replacing its former adherence to the principle of voluntary controls. In tracing the trend towards regulation of health care facility growth on the national level, Curran suggests that it was the AHA's endorsement of the concept that started the general movement away from voluntarism toward regulation.[14]

Curran observes: "the general evidence of failure of voluntary controls has been so great that the mechanism of legally enforced controls, with participation by providers of services, has moved quickly to the front position among most hospital organization people."[15]

By 1971, there were 33 states in varying stages of developing certificate of need legislation. In a survey conducted that year, it was reported that during the years 1966 through 1971, a total of 52 bills had been introduced or reintroduced in state legislatures, of which 14 had been enacted, nine had failed to pass, and the remainder were pending.[16]

By the end of the legislative year 1972, there were certificate of need laws covering some category of health care facilities in 20 states, while in 17 states similar bills had been defeated, and by 1973 the number of states with such laws reached 24. However, during that same year, the North Carolina Supreme Court found that state's certificate of need law unconstitutional. It was repealed soon after and the number was reduced to 23. [17]

Curran's analysis of the types of facilities covered, provisions for minimum capital expenditure required, minimum change in bed complement needing review and approval, and changes in service under certificate of need legislation shows variation from state to state. [18] However, most include all licensed hospitals and nursing homes, as defined by law. (New Jersey has the broadest definition, including health maintenance organizations.)[19]

Despite differences in statutory language, in administrative responsibility, in coverage and limitations, and in procedures for the complex review process, the intent apparently is the same in each jurisdiction. Curran summarizes it this way:

> All of the certificate-of-need legislation has passed through the legislatures on the constantly reiterated promise that they will reduce the costs of hospitalization . . . and will bring rational planning to the health care facilities field. [20]

Most state certification of need programs characteristically involve various levels of review. For example, many states start with an initial review of applications at the areawide level by comprehensive health planning (CHP) units. With few exceptions, their role is advisory, and consumers as well as providers are involved in the process. The next level of review is generally the state Comprehensive Health Planning Council, while the central administering agency is often the state Health Department. Therefore, the "final decision on the granting or denial of a certificate of need is generally placed in the regular traditional governmental agency for health."[21] Finally, the majority of these statutes have some provision for public hearings and appeals.

THE PLANNING-REGULATION DICHOTOMY

Despite the general acceptance of the certificate of need concept among the legislators of some states and the enthusiasm for the notion that the regulatory powers provided to planning agencies under such programs are appropriate and necessary, these points of view are by no means universally held.

Clark Havighurst, for example, raises many questions regarding the certificate of need approach, suggesting that an examination of the experience of other industries under similar legislative programs might demonstrate the potential weaknesses and pitfalls inherent in such

regulatory mechanisms. Franchising and certificate of need laws can
lead to "protectionist tendencies . . . and to elimination of both actual
and potential competition as a potentially important check on ineffi-
ciency, unresponsiveness, and other abuses, of a hospital's dominant
market position," and "special privilege, [which] tends to benefit
insiders more often than it does the public, and promotes inefficient
resource allocation." The result, in Havighurst's view, is the reliance
of the health care system on regulatory oversight which inevitably leads
to "political infighting and influence."[22]

This theme is repeated and expanded by Harris Cohen, who calls
for a re-examination of the assumptions underlying the certificate of
need programs.[23] Cohen is one of a number of commentators who
focuses on an increasingly controversial issue, the nature of the relationship between planning and regulation.

On one side are the state legislatures across the country which
seem to have been convinced that "planning with clout" is better than
planning without. Moreover, CHP agencies are becoming increasingly
involved in the review process involving certification of need in states
where such laws exist and in the implementation of Section 1122 of the
Social Security Act, as added by Section 221 of the 1972 amendments
(Pub. L. 92-603).

This trend notwithstanding, questions are being asked about the
appropriateness and desirability of combining planning with regulation
and about the compatability of these functions. For example, Gottlieb
suggests that the "threat" these laws pose to positive health services
development is great and bears careful consideration.[24] He suggests
that the following are at risk where the regulatory mechanism is combined with areawide planning efforts:

1. Long-range planning will not get the proper emphasis because
of the focus on the bricks and mortar aspects of capital development.

2. Positive planning will be threatened because regulation tends
to result in rigidity and operates as a restrictive mechanism. Therefore,
gaps will not be filled.

3. Cooperation between planning units and providers of care, so
difficult to win, may be lost because the regulatory function will generally cause the regulated to view the planning agency as the "enemy."

4. Sensitivity to changes in the environment requiring shifts in
priorities will be reduced and responsiveness lost due to conservatism,
bureaucratization, or political necessity, inevitable in the regulatory
process.[25]

Havighurst agrees that the certificate of need laws "may be
destructive to the best elements of health planning." He states, for
example:

By converting planners into regulators, certificate of need
and franchising laws will alter the politics of health planning

and convert planners from facilitators of better decision-making in voluntary and public hospitals into participants in a political power struggle similar to that which surrounds other regulatory efforts.[26]

In his analysis of the planning-regulation question, Cohen points out that "advocates of functional checks and balances will argue against merging planning with regulation—not because planning would become more politicized—but because the planning role might cease to function altogether.[27]

In a recent report published by the General Accounting Office in which health planning and certificate of need programs were studied in some detail, the following concerns were expressed by authorities participating in the study:

. . . too much emphasis has been placed on regulating and too little on planning, with the result that planning agencies are too often placed in the position of being against proposed actions rather than being for desired actions.[28]

Cohen carries this concept even further, arguing that

. . . in seeking the authority to regulate—or even the author-ity to participate in the regulatory process—as a means of strengthening their role as planners, the CHP agencies merely exchanged one role for another, i.e., a potentially dynamic role as planner for an essentially passive and reactive role as regulator.[29]

During the last decade or more, regulation has increasingly come to be a fact of life in the health industry. The "planning-regulation dichotomy" is an outgrowth of this general trend. As Somers points out,

. . . the health care industry, especially the hospital component, is . . . extensively controlled by both federal and state governments. . . . Few, if any, other industries have been subjected to so much piecemeal and uncoordinated regulation . . . [30]

The ever increasing role of government in the financing of personal health care and in the development of health resources, both manpower and facilities, has caused legislators and the public to require that conditions be attached to these large expenditures of public funds.

Those who advocate the certificate of need approach are convinced that it serves to strengthen the planning function at the areawide and state levels. Those who oppose often seek the same ultimate aims but advocate alternative means for achieving them. Anne R. Somers appears to be correct that the question of "how to regulate" has replaced the former one "should we regulate."[31]

The "public utility concept" has been gaining attention in a number of forums. Beverlee Myers describes the generic principles behind what she calls the "health authority" concept. Myers identifies the objectives of such a mechanism as well as "the authority to be used to achieve the objectives."[32] Five alternative models are analyzed. On the issue of combining planning with regulatory power, Myers is opposed, quoting Havighurst's argument that:

. . . aggressive planning is simply incompatible with the kind of bargaining stance which regulators customarily adopt. Planning requires principles, goals, and an incentive to pursue them, none of which are regulatory agencies given nor do they attempt to develop. Instead they pursue what has been called the "minimal squawk" principle, offending no vocal interest group more than is necessary to mollify another.[33]

Thus, it is clear that powerful arguments may be offered both for and against combining planning with regulatory functions through the certification of need mechanism. An analysis of empirical evidence to either support or refute these arguments seems to be desirable and necessary.

In the analysis which follows, the outcomes of hospital facilities planning for the period prior to the enactment of the certification of need program in New York State will be compared with facilities planning outcomes after implementation of the program. The contrast between "voluntary" planning and planning combined with regulatory powers provided under the certificate of need legislative program will be analyzed and inferences will be drawn based on the New York State experience.

NOTES

1. Preamble to Pub. L. 89-749, The Partnership for Health Act, 1966. Known as the Comprehensive Health Planning Act, it redirected earlier health planning concepts and was viewed as a solution to the problems of the health care system in the United States.

2. Hospital Survey and Construction Act of 1946.

3. For a description of hospital planning both before and after enactment of the Hill-Burton Act, see Joel J. May, Health Planning: Its Past and Potential (Chicago: University of Chicago, 1967); Anne Somers, Hospital Regulation: The Dilemma of Public Policy (Princeton, N. J.: Princeton University, 1969); Symond Gottlieb, "A Brief History

of Health Planning in the United States, " Regulating Health Facilities Construction, Proceedings of a Conference on Health Planning, Certificates of Need, and Market Entry, ed. Clark Havighurst (Washington, D. C.: American Enterprise Institute for Public Policy Research, 1973).

4. See Gottlieb, op. cit., for a more detailed description of the genesis of these health planning agencies.

5. Ibid.

6. See Herman M. Somers and Anne R. Somers, Doctors: Patients, and Health Insurance (New York: Doubleday Anchor and Co., Inc., 1961), pp. 71-79.

7. P. L. 89-749, Comprehensive Health Planning Act of 1966.

8. For an analysis of the rationale for and flaws in the certificate of need approach, see Clark Havighurst, "Regulation of Health Facilities and Services by 'Certificate of Need, '" Virginia Law Review 59, no. 7 (October 1973).

9. William Curran, "National Survey and Analysis of Certificate-of-Need Laws for Health Facilities, " Regulating Health Facilities Construction. Proceedings of a Conference on Health Planning, Certificates of Need, and Market Entry, ed. Clark Havighurst, op. cit., pp. 87-88.

10. May, op. cit., pp. 36-40.

11. Ibid., pp. 35-36.

12. Joint Committee of the American Hospital Association and Public Health Service, Areawide Planning for Hospitals and Related Health Facilities (Washington, D. C.: United States Public Health Service, 1961).

13. May, op. cit., pp. 40-45.

14. Curran, op. cit., pp. 87-88.

15. Ibid., p. 89

16. Peter J. Elsasser and Thomas P. Galinski, "Certificate of Need, Status of State Legislation, " Hospitals 45 (December 16, 1971): 58.

17. Clark Havighurst, "Regulation of Health Facilities and Services by 'Certificate of Need,'" op. cit., p. 1145.

18. Curran, op. cit., pp. 94-95.

19. See Anne R. Somers, "State Regulation of Hospitals and Health Care: The New Jersey Story, " Blue Cross Reports, Research Series 11 (July 1973), for an extensive description.

20. Curran, op. cit., p. 108.

21. Ibid., p. 97.

22. Clark Havighurst, as quoted in Harris Cohen, "Regulating Health Care Facilities: The Certificate of Need Process Re-examined, " Inquiry (September 1973).

23. Ibid.,

24. Symond R. Gottlieb, "Certification of Need: Potential Threat to Planning, " Hospitals 45 (December 16, 1971): 51-58.

25. Ibid.

26. Clark Havighurst, as quoted in Cohen, op. cit., pp. 7-8.

27. Ibid.

28. Comptroller General of the United States. Report to the Con-
gress, "Study of Health Facilities Construction Costs." Joint Committee
Print, 92nd Congress, 2nd Session, U.S. Government Printing Office
(Washington, D.C., 1972), p. 886.

29. Cohen, op. cit., p. 7.

30. Anne R. Somers, "State Regulation of Hospitals and Health
Care: The New Jersey Story," op. cit., p. 2.

31. Ibid.

32. Beverlee A. Myers, "The Health Authority Concept—Is It
Feasible?" Prepared for the Third Annual President-Elect Session of the
American Public Health Association (November 5, 1973, San Francisco,
California), p. 3.

33. Clark Havighurst, as quoted in Myers, op. cit., p. 11.

2

**REGULATION OF
HEALTH FACILITY
CONSTRUCTION IN
NEW YORK STATE**

In 1964, New York State enacted the Metcalf-McCloskey Act (Chapter 730, Laws of 1964).[1] Under the provisions of this law and the superseding 1965 amendments (Article 28),[2] hospital and health related facility construction, or substantial alterations, renovations, and modernization of existing facilities or services, require prior approval from the state commissioner of health.

The New York State certificate of need legislation, as the Metcalf-McCloskey Act and Article 28 have come to be known, established for the first time in the United States a regulatory mechanism which provided "clout" to the health and hospital planning process. One interpretation of the law's purpose is summarized in this passage:

> [It is] a mechanism for ensuring that the health care industry
> shall expand only in accordance with formulated plans that
> seek to ensure accessibility and availability of health care
> to the greatest number of people. [3]

The ultimate responsibility for approving proposed projects is in the hands of the commissioner of health. Before making his final decisions, however, he must consider the recommendations of the State Hospital Review and Planning Council and the regional agency in whose jurisdiction the project will be located. In the case of establishment of new facilities, the Public Health Council has authority to approve or disapprove proposed projects.

Following is a brief summary of highlights in the development of the certification of need program in New York State. Included also is a description of its purposes as well as the major provisions embodied in the law.

HISTORICAL DEVELOPMENT

The certificate of need legislation was not New York State's first official effort to establish a health and hospital planning function, nor was it the earliest attempt to regulate health facilty construction. By the time the Hospital Survey and Construction (Hill-Burton) Act was enacted in 1946, New York had already established a Board of Social Welfare and a Public Health Council to advise the state on matters relating to social welfare and public health.

Landmark surveys of hospitals and health care facilities had been conducted in New York City in the 1920s and 1930s, and voluntary health planning agencies (the Hospital Council of Greater New York and the Council of Rochester Regional Hospitals) had been established before 1940. With passage of the Hill-Burton program, however, health and hospital planning gained special importance.

In 1948, the governor appointed a Joint Hospital Survey and Planning Commission, created as an independent agency under New York State law, to administer the Hill-Burton program. The commission, along with the Hill-Burton State Advisory Council, was responsible for development of a state plan and for the allocation of federal grants for hospital construction. Seven regional voluntary planning agencies, including the two already in existence, were given responsibility for the initial review of applications for federal funds under the program.

The state and regional councils made a number of contributions to the planning movement in New York State. Among them were:

1. development of a forum at the local level to plan for hospitals and health facilities

2. surveys and inventories of existing facilities and estimates of needed hospitals, nursing homes, rehabilitation centers, diagnostic and treatment facilities for the region served

3. development in cooperation with the state agency of guidelines and policies regarding size, distribution, and expansion of hospitals

4. establishment of a review process in which applications for federal grants for construction of hospitals and related facilities were evaluated and recommendations for either approval or disapproval were transmitted to the state agency.

Despite these efforts to influence the "size, location and improvements in the availability and quality of needed services,"[4] public criticism of the health care system in New York State was on the rise.

In 1960, two studies were commissioned by the New York State Health Department and the New York State Insurance Department, because of concern over the rising costs of hospital care and hospital insurance rates.[5] The studies were conducted by Ray Trussell and others, then of the Columbia University School of Public Health and

Administrative Medicine. Among the many recommendations was one which called for creation of a State Hospital Review and Planning Commission. Soon thereafter, a number of organizational changes resulted within the New York State Department of Health. For example, the Joint Hospital Survey and Planning Commission became the Health Department's Division of Hospital Review and Planning. At the same time, the New York State Advisory Council, originally created in 1948 along with the Joint Hospital Survey and Planning Commission, became the New York State Hospital Review and Planning Council.

Early in 1963, a bill was introduced in the state legislature by Senator George Metcalf at the request of the Joint Legislative Committee on Health Insurance Plans.[16] Assemblyman Frances McCloskey introduced a similar proposal in the assembly.

According to an article in the New York _Times_, the bill died in committee in part because Governor Rockefeller showed no interest in its passage. Despite this early difficulty, the bill ultimately became law, but not until those who would be most affected by it had the opportunity to analyze and discuss it and make recommendations and counterproposals as to its final form. Those who met in private and commented, often publicly, on the proposed bill included members of state and regional hospital planning councils, the Hospital Association of New York State (HANYS), the Greater New York Hospital Association, Blue Cross plans, industry, and labor. (The peak of pre-enactment activity seems to have occurred in 1963, when planning councils' executive committees and boards of directors kept the Metcalf Proposal high on their agendas, as did the New York Labor-Management Council of Health and Welfare Plans, HANYS, the Blue Cross plans, and others who would be affected by the proposed bill.)

Those who favored the legislation relied heavily on Trussell's extensive reports on the quality, quantity, and costs of medical care. Among the most vocal advocates was John O'Rourke, president of Teamsters Joint Council 16. He was influenced by the section in one of the Trussell studies in which it was reported that 23 percent of the sample of teamster family members had received poor medical care, which care was paid for by the union's trust fund.[17] O'Rourke was not only concerned with quality but also with costs, because in his view, not enough was understood about the influence of new hospital construction on insurance rates.

J. Douglas Coleman, then president of Blue Cross, agreed that there was no orderly process by which the hospital facilities of an area were developed in relation to the true needs of the population of the area.

The proposal was viewed by its advocates as an acceptable approach to regulation of health facilities in the state. In the summary of the provisions of the Metcalf-McCloskey Act, the following reasons were given for the legislative program:

1. the rapidly rising costs of hospital care

2. evidences of construction programs in excess of estimated needs and cases of undesirable duplication of facilities and services

3. the rapid increase in the demand for hospital admissions on the part of the public for both inpatient and emergency room services

4. evidence of overutilization of high-cost inpatient facilities (short-term general hospitals) when patients could be served as well or better in home care programs, or on an ambulatory basis, or in good nursing home facilities

5. the lack of legal controls with regard to the development of new hospitals or the expansion of existing ones.[8]

The Metcalf-McCloskey Bill became law on April 22, 1964 (effective October 1, 1964) and contained provisions for a strengthened review process at the state and regional level.

The role and size of the New York State Hospital Review and Planning Council changed in relation to the New York State Department of Social Welfare and the Board of Social Welfare (then responsible) on matters of licensing, and on new construction and expansion, or substantial modification of existing institutions. Provision was made for public hearings where the state council was not in agreement with regional councils on particular projects. In such cases, the council and the institution had the right to participate.

Provision was also made for legal recognition of the seven regional hospital review and planning councils. The statute provided a definition of conditions for determination of need for new construction, expansion or modification, and described relationships among state agencies, such as the Department of Health and the Department of Mental Hygiene.

Some of the assumptions behind these provisions may be inferred from the summary prepared by the Department of Health which states that success of the program depends on (1) rapid review and processing of applications and architectural plans; (2) recommendations at the state and regional council levels founded on factual information and not "of an arbitrary and capricious nature;" and (3) "the degree to which these recommendations are followed."[9]

In 1964, Governor Rockefeller appointed a citizen's committee, chaired by Marion B. Folsom, "to study the costs of general hospital care in the State, and to make recommendations as to how hospitals may best provide high-quality care at the lowest possible cost."[10] In addition, the committee was asked to examine the roles and responsibilities of the state agencies concerned with hospital care and to make recommendations as to how these responsibilities might most effectively be carried out.

ARTICLE 28—MAJOR PROVISIONS

Based on the initial report summary and its recommendations, presented to the governor in 1965, the legislature enacted Article 28 of the Public Health Law. The committee made over 50 recommendations, many of which were written into the law. They were aimed at "moderating, monitoring, and meeting the cost of hospital care."[11]

The recommended programs consisted of the following major parts:

1. moderating the cost of care by using the hospital and other health facilities more effectively
2. enactment of a state hospital insurance law
3. revisions in the organization, operation, and regulation of hospital prepayment and insurance
4. a new system of reporting the cost of hospital care
5. payment by the community as a whole of various costs of services to the community
6. full payment for hospital care of indigent and medically indigent patients
7. grants and loans to replenish and construct more modern and efficient hospital and other health facilities
8. realignment of responsibilities for hospital care among agencies of state government
9. a "breathing period" in which the foregoing changes can be put into effect without or with only minimal changes in prepayment rates. [12]

These recommendations were discussed in detail in the preliminary report. In the first section, devoted to moderating the costs of hospital care, it was recommended that each service provided in a hospital needed review "to determine whether it can be done better and more economically, and whether it should be done at all." The report goes on to state that "unnecessary hospitals and unneeded beds exist in New York State."[13]

The committee recommended seven approaches to help prevent unnecessary duplication of costly services and equipment and unnecessary hospital construction. They included, among others, conversion of underutilized facilities before new beds are approved, consolidation of some hospitals, conversion of others, and the closing of those found to be unnecessary.

Other recommendations included fuller use of existing facilities, preadmission testing as part of an improved system of ambulatory care programs, the establishment of utilization review procedures within institutions to assure the quality and medical necessity of services provided, alternative care programs for those patients who do not need inpatient services in the short-term general hospital but are not well enough to go home and, finally, effective formulary systems and generic prescribing programs.

Regarding realignment of responsibilities for hospital care among the agencies of state government, the committee noted that "responsibilities for hospital affairs are now scattered among many agencies of New York State. No one agency, nor even the aggregate of agencies, has a comprehensive responsibility for being informed about all aspects of hospitals and related institutions. . . ."[14] To cope with the lack of a state policy on hospitals and the problem of "piecemeal and inadequate" administration of health facilities, the committee recommended that the New York State Health Department become the central state agency for hospital affairs. On the recommendation of the Folsom Committee, most state regulatory functions were transferred from the Department of Social Welfare to the Department of Health (effective February 1, 1966); these functions included regulation of construction for hospitals, nursing homes, and related health facilities. The Board of Social Welfare retained regulatory authority over establishment of new facilities until Article 28 was amended in the late 1960s. These amendments shifted that responsibility to the Public Health Council and became effective in June 1970.

The declaration of policy and statement of purpose of Article 28 reads as follows:

> Declaration of policy and statement of purpose. Hospital and related services of the highest quality, efficiently provided and properly utilized at a reasonable cost, are of vital concern to the public health. In order to provide for the protection and promotion of the health of the inhabitants of the state, pursuant to section three of article seventeen of the constitution, the department of health shall have the central, comprehensive responsibility for the development and administration of the state's policy with respect to hospital and related services, and all public and private institutions, whether state, county, municipal, incorporated or not incorporated, serving principally as facilities for the prevention, diagnosis or treatment of human disease, pain, injury, deformity or physical condition shall be subject to the provisions of this article.

The Department of Health was thus given comprehensive responsibility for the development and administration of the state's health and hospital planning functions, for hospitals and related health facilities, and for services provided therein.

Of greatest interest for purposes of this study are the provisions relating to the prior approval required of the health commissioner for hospital construction.

"Hospitals" were defined very broadly and included not only general hospitals, but also public health centers and a variety of other diagnostic and treatment centers, as well as nursing homes. Excluded were facilities which came under the jurisdiction of the Department of Mental Hygiene.

"Construction" was defined as "the erection, building, or substantial acquisition, alteration, reconstruction, improvement, extension or modification of a hospital, including its equipment."

The law provided that the commissioner "shall not act upon an application for construction of a hospital unless:

a.   The applicant has obtained all approvals and consents required by law . . . and until the council and the regional hospital planning councils concerned have had a reasonable time to submit their recommendations; and

b.   the Commissioner is satisfied as to the public need for the construction, at the time and place and under the circumstances proposed.

In approving construction of hospitals, the commissioner is required to take into consideration the availability of alternative facilities and services which could serve as substitutes for the proposed hospital construction, the need for special equipment in view of existing utilization of comparable equipment in the area, possible economies and improvements in service which might result from centralization and shared services, and finally, the adequacy of financial resources and future sources of revenue.

The act also authorized the State Hospital Review and Planning Council to develop a state hospital code, covering standards for construction and patient care.

Under subsequent amendments, capital financing was made available to nonprofit nursing homes under the Nursing Home Companies Law (Article 28-A) and to hospitals under the Hospital Mortgage Loan Construction Law (Article 28-B).

The source of funding is the New York State Housing Finance Agency which was authorized under these acts to make mortgage loans available to local sponsors, subject to Article 28 review and approval of the commissioner of health.

The legislative intent of Article 28-A (effective September 1, 1966) and Article 28-B (effective January 1, 1970) is summarized in the following excerpts.

Article 28-A
Policy and Purposes of the Article

It is hereby declared that a serious shortage of safe and sanitary nursing home accommodations for persons of low income, whose need for combined nursing care, lodging and board cannot readily be provided by the ordinary unaided operations of private enterprise, exists in many communities throughout the state; that there is a need for nonprofit corporations to construct, with mortgage loan participation by the New York State Housing Finance Agency, low cost nursing home accommodations to meet such needs. . . .

Article 28-B

Policy and Purposes of the Article

Many hospitals and other health facilities throughout
the state are becoming obsolete and are no longer adequate
to meet the needs of modern medicine. As a result of rapid
technological changes, such facilities require substantial
structural or functional changes. Others are unsuited for
continued use by virtue of their location and the physical
characteristics of their existing plants and should be
replaced. . . . It is the purpose of this article to encourage
the timely construction and modernization, including the
equipment, of hospital and other health facilities . . .
with mortgage loan participation by the New York State
Housing Finance Agency. . . .

Review of applications for Article 28-A and Article 28-B mortgage
loans is closely interwoven with the Article 28 review process described
below.

THE REVIEW PROCESS

The review process involves several levels of review and evaluation
before the commissioner of health or the Public Health Council makes
a final decision to approve or disapprove any proposed construction,
expansion, or renovation of a health care facility, or change in program
or services.

A sponsor is required to submit an application to the local regional
planning agency in whose area the project will be located and to the
state Department of Health. The proposed project is reviewed in detail
by each of these reviewing bodies.

Recommendations by the Department of Health and the regional
planning council are then made to the New York State Hospital Review
and Planning Council. Based on the council's own assessment, and on
the recommendations of the regional planning council and staff of the
Department of Health, the state council makes its recommendations to
the commissioner of health. In the case of application for establishment of a new facility, the state council recommendations are sent to
the Public Health Council rather than to the commissioner of health.

Part I of the application is to include information regarding the
type of facility or program involved, the estimated cost, methods of
financing the project, and a description of the operation of the facility
when completed.

Decisions made during the review process are generally based on
the assessment of the criteria listed below. The commissioner or the
council must be satisfied that

1. A public need exists in the time and place and under the circumstances proposed by the sponsors.

2. The sponsors have adequate character and competence to operate such a facility.

3. Adequate finances exist for the creation of the program of health services.

4. The cost for such service will be reasonable in terms of the economic market of the area affected.

Part I of the review process may not exceed a maximum of 120 days. This time period begins with the receipt of the application and extends to the final action by the commissioner or the Public Health Council.

Once Part I of the application has been approved, the sponsor is required to submit Part II within 60 days. Part II of the application provides architectural details of the proposed project and must be approved or disapproved within 30 days of submission. Thereafter, the Department of Health, Bureau of Architectural and Engineering Services, becomes involved, providing consultation services to the sponsor.

Under provisions of Article 28, a sponsor of a project which is disapproved by the commissioner or the Public Health Council may ask for a public hearing. Arguments are heard by an independent hearing officer appointed by the commissioner. The findings, including the reasons for the recommendation of disapproval, are presented by the staff of the regional planning council with jurisdiction in the particular case and by the staff of the State Review and Planning Council. In the event there is disagreement on a particular project between the State Review and Planning Council and a regional planning council, the latter may request a hearing in order to explain and justify its position and recommendations. Similar hearing procedures are available to both sponsors and regional planning councils in cases where the Public Health Council disapproves projects involving establishment of new facilities.

In theory, the opportunity to request a public hearing assumes procedural due process and protects the public interest. William Leavy, director of the Bureau of Health Facility Planning, describes the hearing process as follows: "Through these checks and balances, arbitrary decisions affecting the development of the state's health services are largely avoided."[15]

In practice, the mechanism designed to protect procedural due process was operating either ineffectively or not at all during the early years of implementation. * Moreover, there are no provisions either in

---

*In interviews with Walter Livey and others in the Office of Legal Counsel of the New York State Department of Health, the author of this study was advised that it was only after 1972 that hearings could be scheduled in a timely manner. Before that, there were too few hearing

the statute or in subsequent regulations for the protection of individuals and groups who are affected by approval of new or expanded facilities. Curran finds this a major flaw in the legislation. He observes that

> This is an example of rather myopic legalistic thinking. It assumes that grievances can only arise out of the facilities applicant's own loss of a financial interest in construction or expansion of his property. Actually the central theme of this legislation is the public interest in stopping unnecessary construction. It is when a certificate is granted, not when it is denied, that this interest could be compromised. [16]

NOTES

1. New York Public Health Laws (Chapter 730, Laws of 1964).

2. New York Public Health Laws (Chapter 795, Laws of 1965).

3. Peter J. Elsasser and Thomas P. Galinski, "Certificate of Need, Status of State Legislation," Hospitals 45 (December 16, 1971): 54.

4. Now York State Department of Health, Division of Hospital Review and Planning, "Summary of the Provisions of the Metcalf-McCloskey Bill," mimeographed (November 2, 1964).

5. Ray Trussell and others, Prepayment for Medical and Dental Care in New York State, and Prepayment for Hospital Care in New York State (New York: Columbia University, School of Public Health and Administrative Medicine, 1962).

6. Historical background is based in part on interviews with the Honorable George Metcalf (July 13, 1973), the Honorable Marion Folsom (October 9, 1973), and members of the staff of the New York State Department of Health, Bureau of Facility Planning.

7. Ray Trussell and others, Prepayment for Medical and Dental Care, "A Study of Medical and Hospital Care Received by a Sample of Teamster Families in the New York City Area, Late 1960," op. cit., pp. 225-248.

8. "Summary of Provisions of the Metcalf-McCloskey Bill," op. cit.

9. Ibid.

10. "Report of the Governor's Committee on Hospital Costs," preliminary report (Albany: 1964).

11. "Report of the Governor's Committee on Hospital Costs," final report (Albany: April 9, 1965), p. 5.

---

officers in the department and applicants frequently withdrew their appeals because of the indefinite timing of hearings.

12. Ibid., p. 7.

13. Ibid.

14. Ibid., p. 51.

15. William Leavy, "The Article 28 Story: New York State's National Leadership in Health Facility Planning," mimeographed (1972).

16. William Curran, "National Survey and Analysis of Certificate-of-Need Laws for Health Facilities," Regulating Health Facilities Construction, Proceedings of a Conference on Health Planning, Certificates of Need, and Market Entry, ed. Clark Havighurst, Washington, D.C.: American Enterprise Institute for Public Policy Research, 1973.

3

MAJOR ISSUES
IN EVALUATION

Some observers suggest that any attempt to evaluate the impact of the certification of need program on areawide facilities planning is an enormously difficult and complex, if not impossible, task. Despite the acknowledged difficulties, evaluation seems especially important because of the enactment of similar legislative programs in spite of the scarcity of data about programs already in existence.

Among the assumptions underlying the passage of the New York State laws were:

1. Statutory authority would ensure that construction of health care facilities would occur in accordance with "public need" as defined by these local agencies for their jurisdictions, and would conform to an overall state plan.

2. The traditional voluntary areawide planning process had failed to stop unnecessary construction, expansion, or alteration thought not to be in the public interest.

3. Trends in the desired direction would be encouraged and enhanced by planning combined with "clout."

Basically, these assumptions revolve around the concept that legal authority would strengthen planning for health facilities, thereby making planning more effective.

Questions have been raised as to the validity of these assumptions (see Part I). Has the statutory authority helped planning agencies prevent unnecessary construction and undesirable trends? Is it true that voluntary planning is less effective than planning combined with "teeth"? If there has been an impact which can be attributed to this change in public policy, is it measurable and, if so, what should be measured?

Perhaps the most logical answer to the last question would be outcomes in terms of patient health and satisfaction. These may be viewed as the ultimate validators of effectiveness. Although improved health status would provide final evidence of an improved health system, which is surely the ultimate goal of health planning efforts, problems associated with using this to measure outcome would be formidable. There are problems regarding health facility planning in terms of goal definition, the intangible nature of the planning process, and its susceptibility to the influence created by the participants. There are problems associated with defining, selecting, and measuring indices of health status; and there are difficulties in establishing cause and effect relationships between health planning and health status, given the level of uncertainty in each area and the inability to control the many intervening variables.

As an alternative, an analysis of decision-making in the planning process might be used as a conceptual framework in order to examine, explain, and evaluate the planning activity.

Joseph Peters suggests other alternatives, including (1) an examination of methods, (2) the validation of goals and evaluation of alternative methods for achieving them, (3) an examination of information used in preparation of plans, (4) the assessment of community involvement and acceptance of the planning process, (5) the analysis of financial effects, and (6) the analysis of effects on the distribution of services.[1] Each of these is promising as a line of inquiry.

A review of the literature reveals, however, that there are only a few investigations dealing with hospital planning effectiveness or with the impact of certification of need programs. There are many explanations for this scarcity including continuing discussion about what health and hospital planning is and is not; what its objectives and methods are, and who should be involved; and the number of alternative approaches to evaluation, each with associated problems.

In the following section, recent studies are identified and discussed. Frameworks for evaluating health program outcomes are examined, and the framework chosen for this research is explained.

REVIEW OF THE LITERATURE

A number of studies have been reported in the literature which have a bearing on areawide facility planning, and several recent works examine the certificate of need laws specifically. An extensive analysis of planning-related studies would extend beyond the scope of this work. Therefore, only a selection from those which relate to either areawide facility planning effectiveness or to certificate of need will be discussed here.

Joel J. May, in his 1967 study of health planning, reported one of the few empirical studies designed to assess the impact of health and hospital planning in selected Standard Metropolitan Statistical Areas

(SMSAs).[2] The study has major strengths, among them (1) the identification of the need to systematically measure the areawide planning agency performance, (2) the identification of some of the limits of research because of "non-specific and frequently ambiguous statements" as to the purposes of planning agencies, and (3) the matching of areas where planning agencies had been established with areas where there were none.[3]

Weak points in the May study include (1) failure to attempt to discover perceptions regarding planning agency effectiveness or regarding the need for planning where no formal agency existed, (2) questionable assumptions about the "validity of certain broad criteria for measuring adequacy of health services in an area," and (3) inadequate analysis of other influences which could have affected the outcomes.

In the spring of 1967, a study series entitled Health Facility Planning Council Evaluation Project was undertaken by Darwin Palmiere and others. It was funded by the U. S. Public Health Service which sought to stimulate "evaluative studies of the operation of health facility planning councils."[4] Report Number 4 in the five-part series consisted of an analysis of responses to four questionnaires which had been sent to a sampling of health facility planning council board members and executive directors, and sampling of administrators of short-term hospitals within council jurisdictions, and directors of all state Hill-Burton agencies having areawide health facility council relationships.[5]

The research design appeared to be rigorous, in that issues were clearly identified and weaknesses spelled out in the introduction. The report built on findings of earlier reports in the series and is a contribution to knowledge about subjective attitudes of participants in the health facility planning process.

Despite limitations in the response rate in two of the categories samples (under 50 percent) causing a problem of bias, the report has a wealth of detailed information about perceptions of a variety of aspects of the areawide planning function in the jurisdictions covered. One disappointing problem was the absence of any discussion as to how the researcher assured the validity and reliability of the responses.[6]

In Report Number 5, Palmiere studied and analyzed trends in eight characteristics of short-term hospitals in each of 40 council areas during a twenty-year period.[7] The direction of change before and after creation of the councils was compared. The report contains important information, especially that relating to the absence of "consistent or extensive changes in trend direction which could be associated with creation of the councils."[8] There were, however, many limitations in the study. For example, a large number of councils had not been in existence long enough for their impact to be evaluated. In addition, no attempt was made to measure the results, in terms of numbers and kinds of facilities, against need estimates prepared by the councils for their own jurisdictions.

In an earlier study, Alan E. Treloar and Don Chill evaluated accomplishments of the Hill-Burton program by eliciting opinions of state planners and others.[9] The authors used these data in conjunction with other measures, including an analysis of material from congressional hearings, a study of state plans, and a statistical analysis of trends in 22 states. The description of the research design in the study is limited because of the absence of discussion on the selection process (random or not). No attempt was made to state how representative the samples were. (Samples in some of the categories seemed too small for reliability.) The instruments used for data collection, such as questionnaires or interview schedules, were not included.[10]

Several studies deal specifically with the New York State regulatory program. The first, entitled "The Article 28 Story: New York State's National Leadership in Health Facility Planning," is an attempt to determine "to what extent the state has succeeded in effecting improvements in the health care facility system through the exercise of these programs."[11] After an excellent introduction and chronology of the program's development, the paper provides an analysis of the number and kind of facilities in terms of geographic location in relation to population, as well as according to auspices. The analysis also includes the degree and extent of structural conformance of inpatient facilities with USPHS standards. Other information relates to facility utilization patterns and trends in hospital size. These indicators were examined for 1966, the first year of the program, and compared with information for 1971.

As an attempt to assess the program, a comparison of the starting time with a later time seems especially appropriate and useful. However, there was no apparent attempt to provide a control for the many variables which might have influenced the direction of change. Were these trends apparent before passage of the legislation in question? What other factors might have had an impact on the outcomes besides the regulatory mechanism?

The author does attempt to compare the trends in New York State with those of the nation as a whole. The approach seems useful because it permits a comparison of observed changes in selected variables over time. However, the execution of this aspect of the study left many questions unanswered. Most of the data for the nation as a whole were not available except for hospitals. Even with respect to these data, no mention was made as to the source of the data, to its validity or reliability. Conclusions were drawn based on insufficient evidence, and in general the variables used were probably too gross for reliable judgments. For example, the entire section devoted to admission rates, lengths of stay, and general utilization patterns is open to serious question. These factors are known to be influenced by physician and patient behavior, financial mechanisms, availability of facilities, and a host of other factors which were not taken into account.

The second study is a case history. It contains a good summary of events leading to passage of the certificate of need laws of New York

State as well as a description of the review process. There was no attempt to assess the program, and therefore the study is useful only as a descriptive analysis of the steps in the review process.[12]

Anne Somers has written extensively on hospital regulation in the United States. In a book published in 1969, she pointed out that it was then too soon to evaluate the impact of the new New York State laws.[13] However, she suggested an approach to evaluation by comparing hospital expenditures in New York State with those for the nation as a whole.

In her analysis of the years 1964-67, Somers found that total hospital expenditures rose about 45 percent during that time, while in New York State the rise was "one percentage point less."[14] These figures do not explain their relationship to either health and hospital facilities planning or to the certification of need legislation. It is not clear, for example, whether the lower percentage increase is significant or not. Were total expenditures rising faster in New York State than in the rest of the nation prior to 1964? Would there have been a larger increase if New York had not established the regulatory mechanism?

In her analysis of other cost data, Somers found a different picture. The reverse was true with regard to costs per patient and costs per hospital. She concludes that "the 32 per cent rise in cost per patient day indicates the large cost area that is currently beyond the reach of the planning efforts."[15]

In 1967, Ray Trussell submitted a report to the state commissioner of health on the status of implementation of the recommendations of the Governor's Committee on Hospital Costs.[16] The study was an assessment of the first two years' experience to determine what had been done about the committee's recommendations, including those not mandated by law. The primary focus, of course, was to see "how well the legal mandates have been carried out."[17]

A questionnaire based on the committee's recommendations was distributed by regional councils and by the Columbia University School of Public Health and Administrative Medicine, under the auspices of the state commissioner of health. The responses represented an 85.2 percent return, and much important information was gathered.

Five groups were surveyed:

1. individual hospitals which were further categorized by size
2. regional review and planning councils
3. the State Hospital Review and Planning Council
4. the State Department of Health
5. other state agencies, as well as other organizations, notably insurance carriers and third party payors

The results of the study are spelled out in great detail, providing a scenario of the status of implementation of the recommendations as of 1967. The major weakness of the study is that no mention was made of any attempt to validate the responses to the questionnaires. For

example, the individual hospitals were asked to report whether or not
they had excess acute care beds. They were also asked to describe
how they had tried to improve summer and weekend operations. There
was no attempt in the study to use other available data, beyond those
which were included in the responses to the questionnaires, to evaluate
the validity and reliability of the answers.

As stated in Chapter 1, Harris Cohen, in his recent article in
Inquiry, examines some basic assumptions underlying this area of public
policy.[18] Cohen raises questions regarding the concept of "need,"
suggesting that the criteria used in such determinations are often vague
and subjective. Further, he argues that responsiveness of the decision-
makers to political pressures exists and should be recognized. The
relationships between the regulated and the regulatory process are
explored as well as the problem of combining the planning function with
the regulatory process. Finally, Cohen calls for a better understanding
of who makes the decisions and on what basis. He points out that the
participants in the process wear many hats and are often members of
"competing constituencies" precluding objectivity in decisionmaking.[19]

George Steuhler, reporting on the Maryland experience with
certificate of need, provides an interesting analysis of the legislative
program, its constraints, and a number of major and as yet unresolved
issues.[20] Using a "systems analysis" approach, the author evaluates
the program's impact, focusing primarily on actions taken (approval or
disapproval) during the review process. There was no attempt, however, to test the author's assumption that the results of these actions
would "more effectively and efficiently meet community needs and con-
tribute to a comprehensive health care system."[21]

In the following section, various approaches to evaluation are
described and the framework selected for this study is explained.

APPROACHES TO EVALUATION

Recent interest in the evaluation of public policy has resulted in
development of a number of models, strategies, and other theoretical
frameworks for analysis. David C. Caputo devised a model for evaluating urban public policy which allows "feedback" and information
exchange, permitting "mid-course" corrections and adjustments.[22] A
significant aspect of his model is the provision for involvement of both
citizen groups and professionals in an ongoing evaluative process.

In the Administrative Science Quarterly, Thomas T. Cook and
Frank P. Scioli described the theory and application of what they called
"A Research Strategy for Analyzing the Impacts of Public Policy" in an
article so entitled.[23] The authors review the literature relating to the
systems approach to program evaluation, but recommend an alternate
framework to those currently in use. Their purpose in developing the

strategy is well summarized in their quote from the well known social
scientist Mowitz:

> Policy analysis has seldom followed through to examine
> the impacts of the policy decision once made. The most sig-
> nificant piece of information for the good of society is lacking,
> that is, did the policy trigger a chain of events dealing effec-
> tively with the substantive problems at which the program was
> aimed. [24]

The authors applied their theoretical framework to a study and
analysis of public policy in the area of air pollution in the United States,
using a multivariate factorial design, an approach which seems especially useful in an attempt to analyze the impact of a complex public
policy program in a rapidly changing environment over a given time
period. It seems to allow for "partitioning the total amount of observed
change. "[25]

Lynn D. Deniston, Irwin M. Rosenstock, and Vlado A. Getting
view evaluation in terms of attainment of program objectives, each of
which implies one or more necessary conditions, termed "sub-
objectives, " which must be accomplished. Activities are performed
and resources are expended to support program performance. Their
model employs systematic descriptions and measurement of three
variables: resources, activities, and objectives. [26]

Medical care evaluation has recently emerged as a separate area of
inquiry. According to Avedis Donabedian, such evaluation may be
accomplished through analysis of process, structure, or outcomes. [27]
While this approach was developed specifically for appraisal of quality
of care and utilization review activities within medical care settings,
the framework has applicability and is being used in other types of
evaluative research. For example, current efforts to evaluate CHP
agency effectiveness focus on structure and process. [28] Other researchers rely heavily on this model to analyze and evaluate the effectiveness
of health planning.

In Douglas R. Brown's study, for example, process was the framework for analysis. [29] Planning was viewed as incremental and appeared
to be a goal in itself. Brown based his conclusions on observations and
results of interviews with 75 staff planners in 30 health and hospital
facility planning agencies.

There are weaknesses in the Brown study. For example, there is
no discussion of interviews with providers of care or with other participants in the planning process, including members of the councils'
boards of trustees. One pertinent set of findings, however, related to
the following perceptions regarding evaluations of the process:

> [A] very interesting output often cited by planners involves
> the number of hospital beds approved and disapproved in the

review processes, and the number of unnecessary hospital
bed projects blocked by the council.

> . . . [planners] take special delight when they are success-
> ful in holding down the number of beds "not conforming to
> community needs."

> . . . most of the councils illustrate as evidence of their
> progress the fact that they have been responsible for pre-
> venting or discouraging the construction of so many beds. . . .

> . . . except for a few of the planners who are located in
> regions where the need for more short-term hospital beds is
> quite apparent most of the planners are sure that their coun-
> cil has been more or less successful in keeping down the
> number of newly constructed beds of this type.

> . . . [F]ailures cited by the planners usually are considered
> to be rather important in the development of a logical health
> care system in their community. . . .[30]

Brown goes on to describe an example of one such failure, the
construction of a new hospital based on "political machinations and
failure on the part of responsible agencies . . . to marshal the necessary power to offset the decision."[31] Other cases of failure were
those where hospitals "ignored the recommendations of the council and
proceeded--most often to build acute care beds."[32]

While structure and process have gained much recent attention,
measuring outcomes of health services and programs has itself emerged
as a central focus in medical care research. For example, in a recent
series of conferences on health services outcomes, the participants
reviewed "the present state-of-the-art of measurement and evaluation
of the effects, or outcomes, of health care services."[33]

The conference was invitational, and investigators who attended
were concerned with the development of criteria for measuring outcomes,
not only those relating to the health status of persons served, but also
those involving volume of services provided, cost-effectiveness of
services, and quality. An especially interesting problem addressed
was that relating to the "most desirable framework for outcomes
measurement." Lester Breslow observed, for example, that

> all health services research takes something as its end-point--
> health status, efficiency, economy or something else; we're
> concerned with the problem of finding some framework, some
> orderly arrangement, into which, we hope, all of the outcomes
> with which we will be concerned can be placed; we're not
> trying to find only the most important or the highest priority

because we recognize there is no such. Depending on the
particular problem or decision or situation out of which the
research grows, a different outcome will be taken as end-
point.[34]

The particular situation which led to the research described here
was the perceived need for regulatory authority to help enforce planning
recommendations and to achieve a more rational distribution of needed
facilities and services. The outcomes chosen and described in the following sections therefore seem logical and appropriate for the purposes
of this research.

In a separate discussion of the outcomes measurement concept,
Paul Densen suggests that "the form of the outcome has to be known;
that is to say, the subject matter under scrutiny has to be such that it
is appropriate to the problem whose resolution is being sought, albeit
sometimes indirect."[35]

The problem whose resolution was being sought in this case was
the spiralling cost of health, especially of hospital care, which was
attributed to the unnecessary duplication of inpatient facilities. This
research is aimed at determining how effectively the certification of
need program worked in curtailing hospital construction not thought to
be needed in the particular areas under study. It is recognized that
there may be only an indirect relationship between unneeded facilities
and costs. An evaluation of that relationship poses special problems
in economics and is therefore excluded from this study. Further, it is
suggested here that a more basic question has to be asked and answered
before such economic analysis is undertaken. Before determining
whether holding down unnecessary construction had had an impact on
costs, it must first be established that changes in the desired direction
have occurred, namely, that unnecessary construction has been held
down.

Sam Shapiro, in discussing the outcomes framework, states that
"[I]mplicit in the issue of outcome is the need to make comparisons.
This may be directed at contrasts between the system and another
setting or between alternative methods within the system or it may
involve change in the system."[36]

Shapiro's comparisons of health status outcomes under two systems of health care are frequently cited in the literature. In the main,
these and subsequent related studies have restricted the application
of the outcomes framework to assessment of health services in terms
of morbidity, mortality, and patient satisfaction. However, several
recent studies apply the outcomes framework to other aspects of
medical care research. For instance, Jonathan Metsch and James
Veney developed a methodology to measure the outcome of consumer
participation. Using content analysis, these investigators grouped
their observations of minutes of consumer board meetings into generic
categories and, using a weighting scale, derived outcome measures
which were used to evaluate particular board actions and activities.[37]

Another example may be found in a new approach to evaluating the "quality of life" as developed by Daniel B. Tunstall of the Statistical Policy Division of the Office of Management and Budget. In a report entitled "Social Indicators 1973," he attempts to establish "statistical indexes of national social well-being" as an aid to policy-making at the national level. Development of yardsticks of progress towards societal goals (health, education, freedom from fear of crime) is the main objective of this approach to statistical display. The following passage appeared in a summary of the project in the New York Times.

> In selecting indicators, the chief emphasis was put on figures measuring end products of the social system. For example, education was measured in terms of children's classroom performance rather than school spending, which is not necessarily related to learning. [38]

The project was developed because economic indicators traditionally used for policy-making fail to describe social progress or program outcomes.

Perhaps the most pertinent documentation of the outcomes approach to evaluation is Roger Noll's analysis of the theory and practice of public utility regulation. [39] Noll describes various models for regulating certain industries and analyzes what he calls "success indicators" and "regulatory outcomes." One of these success indicators is the performance of the regulated industry.

In a section entitled "Empirical Observations on Regulatory Outcomes," Noll points to "some revealing findings about the accuracy" of predictions made under two theoretical constructs regarding the impact of regulation on outcomes. "The traditional view predicts that regulation will cause prices to be lower than they would be without regulation," while the revisionist theory, as he describes it, "has an opposite prediction." Noll then reports on the few empirical studies which examine actual performance in terms of regulatory agency effectiveness. He concludes that "the empirical evidence clearly contradicts the traditional view of regulation." Noll suggests that these empirical observations can mean one of two things:

> either regulation performs no function at all . . . or regulation succeeds not in lowering prices . . . but instead in raising costs so that the potential profitability of monopoly pricing is eroded away. [40]

The analogy here, although not perfect, is clear. Two points of view have emerged regarding the impact of certificate of need legislation on health facility planning, but to date no empirical studies have been conducted to measure "regulatory outcomes."

The framework for this research will be the measurement of outcomes, defined for purposes of this study as observed change in the availability and distribution of inpatient facilities, in relation to the population, in selected geographic areas of New York State during the study period.

NOTES

1. Joseph Peters, Evaluating the Planning Process in Health Care Institutions (Chicago: American Hospital Association Institute, 1971).

2. Joel J. May, Health Planning: Its Past and Potential (Chicago: University of Chicago, Center for Health Administration Studies, 1967).

3. Ibid.

4. Darwin Palmiere and others, Health Facilities Planning Council Evaluation Project (Public Health Service, Health Services and Mental Health Administration, 1971).

5. Darwin Palmiere and others, Participant Assessment of Health Facilities Planning Councils, Report Number 4 (1971).

6. Ibid.

7. Palmiere and others, Report Number 5 (1971).

8. Ibid.

9. Alan E. Treloar and Don Chill, Patient Care Facilities: Construction Needs and Hill-Burton Accomplishments (Chicago: American Hospital Association, 1961).

10. Ibid.

11. William Leavy, "The Article 28 Story: New York State's National Leadership in Health Facility Planning," mimeographed (1972).

12. Jay Hersch, "A Case Study of Cost Containment: The State of New York," mimeographed (1973).

13. Anne R. Somers, Hospital Regulation: The Dilemma of Public Policy (Princeton, N.J.: Industrial Relations Section, Princeton University, 1969).

14. Ibid., p. 147.

15. Ibid.

16. Ray Trussel, Status of Implementation of the Recommendations of the Governor's Committee on Hospital Costs (New York: Columbia University, 1967).

17. Ibid.

18. Harris Cohen, "Regulating Health Care Facilities: The Certificate of Need Process Re-examined," Inquiry (September, 1973): 3-9.

19. Ibid.

20. George Steuhler, Jr., "Certification of Need—A Systems Analysis of Maryland's Experience and Plans," American Journal of Public Health (November, 1973): 966-72.

21. Ibid.

22. David C. Caputo, "Evaluating Urban Public Policy: A Developmental Model and Some Reservations," Public Administration Review 33, no. 2 (March/April, 1973), pp. 111-18.

23. Thomas T. Cook and Frank P. Scioli, Jr., "A Research Strategy for Analyzing the Impacts of Public Policy," Administrative Science Quarterly 17, no. 3 (September, 1973).

24. Ibid., p. 329.

25. Ibid.

26. Lynn D. Deniston, Irwin M. Rosenstock, and Vlado A. Getting, "Evaluation of Program Effectiveness," in Herbert C. Shulberg, Alan Sheldon, and Frank Baker (eds.), Program Evaluation in the Health Fields (New York: Behavioral Publications, 1969).

27. Avedis Donabedian, Medical Care Appraisal—Quality and Utilization, a Guide to Medical Care Administration, vol. 2 (New York: American Public Health Association, 1969).

28. The comptroller general of the United States, Report to the Congress, "Comprehensive Health Planning as Carried Out by State and Areawide Agencies in Three States" (1974).

29. Douglas R. Brown, "The Areawide Hospital Planning Process," (Dissertation, Cornell University, 1971).

30. Ibid., pp. 250-63.

31. Ibid.

32. Ibid.

33. Sam Shapiro, "Opening Comments on Outcome Measures," University Medical Care Programs, evaluation papers presented at a conference sponsored by Harvard Center for Community Health and Medical Care, and the National Center for Health Services Research and Development (1971).

34. Ibid.

35. Ibid.

36. Ibid.

37. Jonathan Metsch and James E. Veney, "A Model of the Adaptive Behavior of Administrators to the Mandate to Implement Consumer Participation," Medical Care 12, no. 4 (April 1, 1974): 338-50.

38. Robert Reinhold, "U. S. Report Sums Up Main Social Trends," The New York Times (February 17, 1974), p. A-63.

39. Roger G. Noll, "The Consequences of Public Utility Regulation of Hospitals," mimeographed (undated), p. 13.

40. Ibid.

4

RESEARCH DESIGN
AND METHODOLOGY

STATEMENT OF THE PROBLEM

A modification of the pretest-posttest model of experimental design was used in this study because it controlled for conditions prior to implementation of the certificate of need law. That is, the major methodological question in this study could be framed as follows: Can it be shown that there were measurable differences in the hypothesized directions before and after the new law became effective? To study effects before and after an event such as a policy change requires sufficient data to provide stability to the estimated parameters. In this case the latter concerned planning and population variables common to counties in New York State. Five-year aggregates of data were decided upon. Therefore, the period 1960 to 1965 was used as the preimplementation period. There are strengths and weaknesses in this strategy. Through aggregation of data a mean in a five-year secular trend was obtained. For example, where a particular characteristic—such as change in the number of newly built long-term beds—was small in a given year, by aggregation any confounding effects would be minimized; and yet that data point would be given its due weight in the analysis. The time interval from 1965 to 1970 was considered the post-implementation period.

In this study a time period extending beyond 1970 was avoided because new cost control legislation became effective in New York State in that year. Further, the Economic Stabilization Program was implemented late in 1971 at the national level. Sorting out the influence of these programs on hospital and health facility planning poses many problems. In order to keep these confounding variables from entering into the analysis, 1970 was therefore considered a reasonable cutoff date.

SAMPLING: COUNTIES AND REGIONS

Counties were chosen as the basic study units because they are used in New York State as the basis for virtually all planning activity. The Policy and Procedures Manual developed by the state health department's Bureau of Facility Planning states that the 62 counties "conform with the land use, transportation, and physical development plans of the State and the Governmental structure of the State."

In addition, population and other data are aggregated on a county basis. Moreover, county governmental units, especially county health departments, are a source of health and social services, and often are responsible for direct operation of health facilities.

The county is also used as a basic geographic unit under other legislative programs. A recent example is the case of proposed regulations with respect to establishment of appropriate areas for Professional Standards Review Organizations (PSROs) under Title XI of the 1972 amendments to the Social Security Act (Pub. L. 92-603). The guidelines in the Federal Register (December 20, 1973) specify: "In general, an area should not divide a county. . . . "

The areas designated are based on county groupings except in states and territories where there are too few physicians and the entire state is designated as a single area for PSRO purposes.

Most important is the fact that the state Health Department has consistently used the county for hospital and health facility planning purposes throughout the study period, which makes it possible to conduct a comparative study such as the one described here.

The use of the county as a basic study unit poses one problem. There is considerable mobility of patients between counties seeking health and hospital care. In New York County (Manhattan) this is particularly true. Despite the pattern of intercounty mobility, it was found during a one-day census conducted by Blue Cross in the years 1961, 1964, 1967, and 1971, that, on the average, 81 percent of the patients in hospitals were residents of the same county in which they were hospitalized. Therefore, the county appears to be a reasonable unit of study for purposes of this investigation.

The 25 counties chosen for study appear to be representative of the entire state in some respects. In order to examine the characteristics of all counties, population size and population rate of change during the study period were plotted.

The distribution of all counties showed a dichotomy in terms of population size. Fifty-two of the state's 62 counties may be represented by a line on a probit graph which indicated they were part of a group which may be described as normal. The ten remaining counties appeared to form a separate universe. A corresponding graph drawn for the study counties shows the same pattern. It should be noted, however, that eight of the state's ten most populated urban and suburban

TABLE 4.1

Percent of Patients Hospitalized in Same County as
Place of Residence

Region County	Year			
	1961	1964	1967	1971
New York City				
New York	55.6	55.2	52.6	53.2
Bronx	79.6	80.9	79.3	80.3
Kings	89.0	90.1	88.8	90.1
Queens	82.7	83.2	85.4	82.9
Richmond	55.6	58.3	60.5	72.8
Northern Metropolitan				
Dutchess	84.5	83.7	77.5	73.5
Orange	87.3	87.6	84.2	80.7
Putnam	71.9	58.7	81.7	69.8
Rockland	87.9	87.4	89.0	88.3
Sullivan	89.8	92.5	89.2	90.5
Ulster	94.7	91.6	95.0	90.9
Westchester	88.5	89.1	88.3	87.7
Long Island				
Nassau	87.3	84.4	82.4	83.0
Suffolk	90.7	91.3	90.7	92.5
Average	81.2	81.0	81.7	81.2
Range	55.6-94.7	55.2-91.6	52.6-95.0	53.2-92.5

Source: Blue Cross/Blue Shield of Greater New York.

counties are included among the 25 study counties. The 17 remaining study counties are distributed evenly among all New York counties, 13 of which may be included among the 37 rural counties in the state. Therefore, the 25 study counties may be taken to represent the wide diversity found among all counties of the state with respect to population size.

Changes in population size are also noteworthy. An analysis of percent change during the years 1960 to 1970 reveals that all but three counties may be represented by a single normal distribution depicting rates of change. However, those three counties, all of which are included in the study sample, show a growth rate so different from the rest that they must be considered separately. The remaining study counties are scattered among all the counties of the state with respect to percent change in population.

Thus, the study counties seem to represent the wide diversity in population change which characterized the ten years under study. An examination of these trends in population growth or loss is important because of the intent of the certificate of need legislation. Assuring distribution of hospital and health facilities according to need was a major objective, as was curtailment of duplication of costly inpatient facilities and overbuilding of unneeded facilities. The analysis which follows focuses on the outcomes of the planning process in the broad spectrum of counties: those represented by a rapid positive change in the population, and presumably in the demand for health and hospital services; those characterized by moderate change as well as counties showing a slow growth rate, or an outmigration, as was the case in parts of New York City.

Four hospital service regions have been selected for study: New York City, the Rochester region, the northern metropolitan region, and Long Island. Within these regions are 25 counties which serve as the basic study units for this investigation.

The reasons for selection of these hospital service regions include the fact that two of the four regional hospital councils had been among the oldest in the nation. It is assumed, therefore, that observed change in facility planning outcomes will not have been influenced by the absence of a planning capability and could be attributed to the change in public policy being studied. It should be noted that both the Long Island and the northern metropolitan area did not have independent staff planning capability but were served by the staff of the Health and Hospital Planning Council of Southern New York, Inc. during most of the study period.

Need estimates had been developed by the regional health planning councils and the state Health Department for each county of the state during the study period. Observed changes within the four planning regions chosen for study are examined in relation to these need estimates. However, no attempt is made to validate the estimates which are taken as given. While it is recognized that estimating need for inpatient facilities is a complex and difficult task, and that such

Hospital Service Regions of New York State

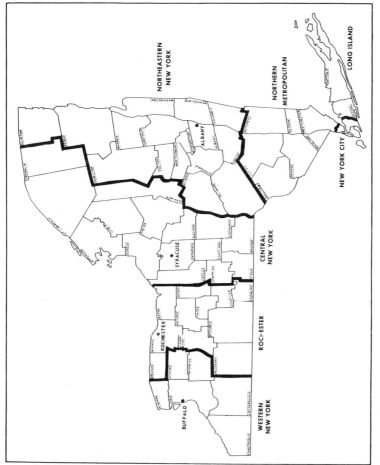

Source: New York State Department of Health, 1965-66.

41

estimates change over time, the focus of this study is not to question the methods used for arriving at such estimates but rather to evaluate whether the regulatory authority has helped the planning agencies and the state fulfill what have been thought to be the needs of the state and local communities.

DATA COLLECTION

The data were collected at official and voluntary planning offices from records and data collected for purposes other than those in this study (secondary analysis). In the instance of each organization and agency, permission was obtained from the appropriate person or persons before data were collected. Good working relationships were established in each place. One of the personally rewarding features of this study was the enthusiastic response to the explanation of the study's objectives. Virtually all doors were opened and considerable assistance was given the study and its data collection.

Sources

As expected, there were many sources of data needed in order to estimate the variety of population and planning parameters required by the study. The list below includes the principal sources used.

1. the Laws of New York State
    Chapter 730 (Laws of 1964)
    Chapter 735 (Laws of 1965) Public Health Laws Article 28
2. census reports
3. Municipal Year Book (annual, Washington, D.C.: International City Management Association)
4. Book of the States
5. Health Department inventory of licensed facilities
6. Hill-Harris program data
7. Hospital Guide Issue for years under study (Journal of the American Hospital Association)
8. special studies
9. Health Facility Planning Council Information
    history
    statement of purposes and goals
    written criteria and standards
    estimates of need for inpatient facilities
    staffing pattern
    financing
10. other sources of data
    personal interviews

questionnaires
observation of planning council, board, and committee
  meetings
observation of public health council meetings

Population and Planning Variables

Appendix A contains the independent variables used in the study to characterize the counties. This list was not ideal, but rather one that was possible. For example, because of changes in the survey methods used by the American Medical Association for collecting data between 1965 and 1970 on physicians in various types of practice (that is, solo, partnership, surgical specialty, and so forth) only nonfederal physicians could be included. In general, however, the variables used do represent the concepts considered essential, and in a way that does not seem to invalidate the purposes inherent in their selection.

LIMITATIONS OF THE DATA

There are a number of limitations in this research which need to be made explicit so that subsequent inferences and conclusions drawn can be tempered appropriately. Four principal areas will be reviewed and their inherent research and methodological problems examined: (1) limitations imposed by the research design; (2) the influence of unmeasured variables and covariables, as well as the problem of association versus causality; (3) measurement, validity and data reliability; indices used; and (4) social, historical, political and other variables not studied but which undoubtedly would help explain study findings.

Limitations Associated with the Research Design and Methodology

Certain specific outcomes were selected as dependent variables for the research design. Their specificity was dictated primarily by convention, that is, the general agreement that the law was intended to affect growth of hospital beds. This "bottom line" approach can be criticized as ignoring many intervening variables related to the law's process or its implementation. The latter two kinds of data were not readily available, thus were deemed less suitable for this study. Additionally, earlier studies had used hospital beds, thereby providing a source of comparison.

Costs were not included among the outcome measures because special economic analysis would have been required. Instead, it was assumed that changes observed in general care and long-term care beds, especially when measured against "estimated need," would show what impact the program had, if any, on achieving desired end results with respect to these types of facilities.

Excluded from the study categories were federal and state hospitals, rehabilitation and diagnostic centers, and home health agencies. Further, alternatives to impatient facilities, such as ambulatory care and home care programs, were not included in the analysis.

No attempt was made to validate the need estimates published in the state plans and used in the analysis although it is recognized that, among planning activities, estimating bed needs is a complex and inexact science. Scholars have devoted much attention during the past half century to problems of forecasting bed needs, noting the variety of factors affecting them: predicting utilization patterns, population shifts, changes in demand due to changing patterns of financing care, emerging patterns of medical practice, and new perceptions and attitudes regarding health needs. Moreover, these tend to be interrelated. Commentators have questioned the methods used by the state Health Department for estimating bed needs and have criticized the use of current utilization patterns for predicting future needs. It has been pointed out, for example, that this method does not recognize the existence of the problems of overutilization or misutilization, especially of short-term general care hospitals, thus introducing a confounding factor. Further, quality is not taken into account, nor is the problem of levels of acuity of patients' illnesses addressed. To equate all beds ignores these problems. For purposes of this study we have had to assume that such qualitative factors tend to occur in offsetting directions, thereby minimizing bias.

The before-after study design was selected because it offered a prelaw control period as well as a postimplementation period of the same duration. Each county was its own control, allowing an examination of the impact of the legislation introduced. However, there were major social, economic, and political events during the mid-1960s which may have had a great impact on the outcomes attributed to the introduction of the certificate of need program. Further, the year 1970 was considered the appropriate cutoff time because the New York State cost-control legislation, enacted in 1969, was implemented then, introducing a confounding variable. However, it is understood that capital construction projects such as those being measured here require many years from the initial planning stage to actual completion. Therefore, in using the estimates prepared by the state Health Department, those facilities planned and under construction were counted as well as those in existence at the time of the state survey.

There was an apparent reluctance on the part of the planning councils in the early years after introduction of the certification of need program to disapprove project applications. It was not until after 1970, for example, that there were wholesale disapprovals of applications thought not to be in the public interest. Indeed, in New York City a moratorium was declared on new short-term hospital bed construction, but not until 1972. Therefore, judgment about the full impact of the program should be reserved until other research has been conducted based on a longer time period than was used in this study.

Unmeasured Variables and Associated Problems

In specifying variables in any complex study, choices must be made based on the author's conception and understanding of what will be important or useful for analytical purposes. Errors of omission or commission are inevitable. It is recognized, therefore, that these study results are limited because of the exclusion from the analysis of unmeasured variables, such as certain utilization and demographic data, as well as cost and insurance variables.

The specification of independent variables presented problems in that variables thought to be important could not be included due to unavilability of data. For example, except for Medicare data, information on hospital insurance was either incomplete or nonexistent at the county level.

Where information was available—as in the case of the number of physicians, by county, during the years under study—assuring reliability became a major problem because of changes in the methods used for collecting information on physicians according to their practice specialty. Therefore, the only reliable measure was total number of nonfederal physicians, a limiting factor.

There are other limitations in the use of quantitative methods for analysis of program impacts in that they do not permit examination of the impact on attitudes or on the planning process per se. It has been suggested, for example, that the attitude of institutional planners has changed because of the very existence of the certificate of need requirements, and that this has been more apparent during the past three or four years than at any other time since introduction of the legislation. Interestingly, recent Article 28 applications have tended to be aimed more at replacement of obsolete facilities or construction of ambulatory care units than at expansion of bed capacities.

The total effect of the law was not measured in this study. The emphasis in health planning has shifted away from facilities planning and has moved towards patient care programs and services, both at the institutional and area-wide levels. These changes could be documented through systematic study but would require a different research methodology and design from the one used in this investigation.

It must be stated finally that the variables chosen may be highly correlated with each other but that the association does not necessarily imply causality. Moreover, two or more variables which show a high correlation with each other may in fact be associated with a third but unmeasured variable.

Validity and Reliability of the Data

    While it was possible to obtain information on the number and kinds of general care and long-term facilities in New York State from a variety of sources, it was important to use the most complete set of data available.

    The New York State plans for construction of hospital and related facilities for 1960, 1965-66, and 1970 provided the basic data from which the following were derived:

1. change in the number of general care beds
2. change in the number of long-term care beds
3. number of nonconforming general care beds
4. number of nonconforming long-term care beds
5. percent of need met for general care beds
6. percent of need met for long-term care beds

This source was selected because state plans had been prepared by health department staff for each of the years under study, containing a wealth of useful data, arranged by region and county; the data were based on information maintained in the health department files, including their inventory of licensed health facilities throughout the state; further, the information was consistent from the beginning of the study period until the end in terms of format and level of detail, allowing comparison to be made with respect to such information as bed capacities, types of control, number of beds upon completion of construction under way, and number of beds conforming to USPHS standards for fire-resistiveness. It should be noted that in 1965-66, the "conformity" determination was changed to include fire-resistiveness and fire-safety, and adequacy of nursing units. However, by using the data classification which pertained only to fire-resistiveness, it was possible to keep the 1965-66 data reasonably consistent with 1960 data used in the analysis.

    In the case of long-term care facilities, a slightly different method of categorization was used by the health department in 1960 from that in 1965 or in 1970. For example, in 1965, chronic hospitals were grouped together with nursing homes to comprise the long-term category. Rehabilitation units were excluded in 1965, but by 1970 they were included. For that reason, in gathering data on long-term care facilities, the author examined the data on each facility and included only those which could be classified as nursing homes and chronic care hospitals, excluding from each tally others such as rehabilitation units.

Historical, Political, and Social Factors

The evolution of health planning in New York State and elsewhere has reflected social and political forces which have influenced and been influenced by the nature of the process and the participants, as well as public expectation as to what could be accomplished through such activities. Historically, problems have been identified which seem to defy resolution despite the attempt during each new era of health planning to solve them. As an example, the preface to a major study entitled The Hospital Situation in Greater New York states the following:

> The present volume is the report of a study of hospital conditions in New York City. The survey was undertaken because of the rapid growth of hospital accommodations, a growth unguided by a community policy concerning the need of further services and the better adjustment of existing facilities to the requirements of the metropolis. We have in New York City a farrago of hospital services, excellent and mediocre, large and small, expensive and gratuitous, general and special. Until recently there was no agency in the City which was fully conversant with the facts in the situation.

The study was conducted by E. L. Lewinski-Corwin[1] in 1924 but seems to present a picture not too different from what exists a half century later.

The growth of hospital accommodations within the framework of a "community policy" still presents a problem—thus the perceived need for planning and regulation. We will have the farrago of hospital services and there is still "no one agency . . . fully conversant with the facts . . . " On the contrary, there are a number of agencies which are now involved in various aspects of health planning and development in New York State which represent different interests (and therefore constituencies). Examples include CHP agencies, Article 28 agencies, urban planning units, health departments, and so forth, which in many instances do not cover the same geographic boundaries within a particular area.

A study of the political processes which have influenced the evolution of these agencies and their functions would no doubt shed light on the findings of this study.

NOTE

1. E. L. Lewinski-Corwin, The Hospital Situation in Greater New York, New York Academy of Medicine (New York: Putnam's, 1924).

ANALYSIS OF
BEFORE-AFTER
DIFFERENCES IN GENERAL
CARE AND LONG-TERM
CARE BEDS

5

**GENERAL CARE AND
LONG-TERM CARE FACILITIES
BEFORE AND AFTER
CERTIFICATE OF NEED**

OBSERVED CHANGE IN GENERAL CARE FACILITIES

In 1970, at the end of the study period, there were in existence or planned and approved for construction, fewer but larger general care hospitals in each of the four study regions than there were in 1960.* The one exception was Long Island where the number of general care hospital facilities increased from 30 to 37 between 1960 and 1965 but decreased again to 32 by 1970. This general trend toward larger but fewer units was as evident during the years 1960 to 1965, before the enactment of the certification of need program, as it was during the first five years after its implementation. For example, in the New York City region the number of general care hospitals declined from 143 in 1960 to 134 in 1965. That number dropped to 124 by 1970. In the Rochester region, the number of general care facilities dropped from 32 to 30 during 1960-65 and remained constant between 1965 and 1970, while in the northern metropolitan region there was a decrease of one facility between 1960 and 1965 and of two during the period 1965 to 1970, as shown in Table 5.1.

The average size of general care hospital units in the study regions was larger at the end of the study period than at the beginning. Here again, the trend was evident both before and after implementation of the certification of need program, as seen in Table 5.2.

It is interesting to note that in 1960 there were 33 general care hospital units with fewer than 50 beds, while that number dropped to

*"General care facilities," for purposes of this research, means nonfederal, short-term general and special hospitals, excluding organized tuberculosis, chronic, and nursing home units of general hospitals; state hospitals: diagnostic, rehabilitation, and public health centers.

TABLE 5.1

Number of Facilities for General Care, by Region, 1960-70

Region	1960	1965	1970
Rochester	32	30	30
Northern metropolitan	44	43	41
New York City	143	134	124
Long Island	31	37	32

Source: Compiled by the author.

TABLE 5.2

Average Size of General Care Facilities, by Region, 1960-70

Region	Average No. of Beds per Unit		
	1960	1965	1970
Rochester	128	140	146
Northern metropolitan	139	146	176
New York City	265	286	318
Long Island	136	173	213

Source: Compiled by the author.

18 in 1965. By 1970 there were only 12 general care units of under 50 beds in the study regions. This represented a general decrease in the proportion of small units of under 50 beds in relation to the total number of general hospital facilities in these regions. The most dramatic changes occurred between 1960 and 1965 in the northern metropolitan, New York City, and Long Island regions. Table 5.3 shows changes in the cumulative distribution of general care hospitals by size of unit and by region.

During the period 1960-65 the proportion of general care facilities represented by units of under 50 beds in the three regions mentioned above fell from 25 percent to 12 percent, 19 percent to 5 percent, and 19 percent to 8 percent, respectively. In the period 1965-70 the decrease continued but at a lower rate. In the northern metropolitan area the proportion of under-50-bed units fell from 12 percent in 1965 to 10 percent in 1970, while in New York City it dropped from 5 percent to 3 percent, and in Long Island from 8 percent to 6 percent.

More important, perhaps, is the generally dramatic decrease in the proportion of units of under 100 beds in these three regions during

TABLE 5. 3

General Care Facilities by Size of Unit and Region, 1960-70

Region	1960 Cumulative Percent	No.	1965 Cumulative Percent	No.	1970 Cumulative Percent	No.
Rochester, Total	100	32	100	30	100	30
Under 50 beds	9	3	10	3	7	2
50-99	59	19	63	19	57	17
100-199	75	24	73	22	77	23
200-299	91	29	83	25	87	26
300-399	94	30	93	28	93	28
400+	100	32	100	30	100	30
Northern metropolitan, Total	100	44	100	43	100	41
Under 50 beds	25	11	12	5	10	4
50-99	50	22	44	19	32	13
100-199	80	35	72	31	56	23
200-299	95	42	91	39	83	34
300-399	98	43	100	43	100	41
400+	100	44	--	--	--	--
New York City, Total	100	143	100	134	100	124
Under 50 beds	19	13	5	7	3	4
50-99	29	41	20	27	16	20
100-199	81	75	51	68	45	56
200-299	94	106	72	97	65	80
300-399	97	118	79	106	73	91
400+	100	143	100	134	100	124
Long Island, Total	100	31	100	37	100	32
Under 50 beds	19	6	8	3	6	2
50-99	48	15	27	10	19	6
100-199	81	25	62	23	53	17
200-299	94	29	89	33	78	25
300-399	97	30	95	35	91	29
400+	100	31	100	37	100	32

Source: Compiled by the author.

the study period. For example, in the northern metropolitan region one-half (50 percent) of all short-term general hospital units were under 100 beds in 1960. By 1965, that proportion decreased to 44 percent and by 1970 about one-third (32 percent) of all general care units in the northern metropolitan region contained fewer than 100 beds. In New York City the proportion of under-100-bed units decreased from 29 percent in 1960 to 20 percent in 1965 and to 16 percent by 1970. The trend in the Long Island region was even more dramatic. In 1960, almost half (48 percent) of the general care units contained under 100 beds, while that proportion decreased to 27 percent by 1965 and fell still further, to 19 percent, by 1970.

At the other end of the spectrum, during the years 1960-70 there was a trend toward larger institutions, mainly in New York City. In all study regions there were 29 hospitals of 400 beds or more in 1960, while that number increased to 32 by 1965 and reached 38 by 1970.

During the study period, there were only minor changes observed in the four study regions with respect to the proportion of short-term hospital units under each of three types of control—voluntary nonprofit, local government, and proprietary. Table 5.4 shows these changes. The greatest change occurred in the Long Island region.

In 1960, 55 percent of the 31 short-term hospital units were operated under voluntary auspices and 42 percent were under proprietary control. By 1965, 49 percent of the short-term units were to be found under each of these two types of control. By 1970 the proportion had shifted to 59 percent under voluntary and 38 percent under proprietary auspices. In the other three regions, there were proportionately fewer short-term hospital units under proprietary sponsorship at the end of the study period than at the beginning, but there was no particular change in pattern which could be associated with the introduction of the certification of need program.

In 1970, in three of the study areas, the number and proportion of short-term beds in nonconforming hospitals (specifically in nonfire-resistive structures) was substantially lower than in 1960, although the major change occurred by 1965 (see Table 5.5). In the Long Island region, however, there was an increase between 1965 and 1970 because of a 218-bed short-term hospital which had been judged as conforming in 1960 and 1965 but which did not meet the state Department of Health standards by 1970. (This change is not necessarily associated with different standards but may be the result of more thorough inspection of facilities by the state Health Department.)

In the Rochester region, in 1960, there were short-term beds in nonfire-resistive structures in all but three of the eleven counties. These totalled 420 beds or 10 percent of all short-term beds in that region. By 1965 only three of the eleven counties had short-term beds in such nonfire-resistive structures, amounting to only 87 beds or 2 percent of all short-term beds. By 1970, there were two counties with such nonconforming units, which totalled 48 beds or 1 percent of all short-term beds in the Rochester area.

TABLE 5.4

Percent Distribution of Short-Term Hospital Units, by Region and by Auspices, 1960-70

Region	1960			1965			1970		
	Voluntary	Local Govt.	Propri-etary	Voluntary	Local Govt.	Propri-etary	Voluntary	Local Govt.	Propri-etary
Rochester	88	6	6	90	3	7	87	10	3
Northern metropolitan	77	2	21	79	2	19	80	3	17
New York City	59	12	29	60	14	26	59	14	27
Long Island	55	3	42	49	2	49	59	3	38

Source: Compiled by the author.

TABLE 5.5

Number and Percent of General Care Beds in Nonfire-Resistive Structures, by Region, 1960-70*

Region	1960		1965		1970	
	No.	Percent of Total	No.	Percent of Total	No.	Percent of Total
Rochester	420	10	87	2	48	1
Northern metropolitan	732	13	238	4	286	4
New York City	4,228	11	1,018	3	688	2
Long Island	180	4	137	2	339	5

*For the total number of general care beds in these regions, see Table 5.6.
Source: Compiled by the author.

All counties in the norther metropolitan area contained short-term beds in nonfire-resistive structures in 1960. These units accounted for 732 such beds or 13 percent of all short-term beds in the region. By 1965, only three of the seven counties contained such nonconforming units, which totalled 238 beds or 4 percent of the total. By 1970, there were still nonconforming units in three of the seven counties and in one, Westchester, a hospital judged as conforming during 1960 and 1965 fell short of the standards, therefore accounting for an increase over the 1965 number, but for no increase in percent.

In New York City there were over 4,000 nonconforming short-term hospital beds in nonfire-resistive stuctures in 1960. These represented 11 percent of the total and were distributed among all the counties. By 1965, the number of such conforming units was reduced to 1,018 (less than one-third the number in 1960) and represented 3 percent of the total. By 1970, New York City showed an overall reduction to 688 nonconforming short-term units, which represented 2 percent of the total. Only one county, Richmond, no longer had short-term beds in nonfire-resistive structures by 1965.

Each of the two counties on Long Island contained nonconforming short-term beds throughout the 1960-70 period. In 1960 there were 180 such units representing 4 percent of the total. By 1965 that number was reduced to 137 or 2 percent of the total, but by 1970 there was an increase to 339 which constituted 5 percent of the total. (Of these, 200 were due to a reclassification of formerly conforming facilities.)

General Care Beds

There were an estimated 52,036 general care beds in existence and approved for construction in 1960 in the four study regions. By 1965 that number reached 55,230 and by 1970 there were an estimated 57,797 general care beds in existence or planned. The pattern of change in the number of beds available within each of the study regions shows that the Rochester region and New York City had the smallest increases between 1960 and 1965 (4 percent and 1 percent, respectively), and the same was true for the years 1965 to 1970 (3 percent in each case). In contrast, the northern metropolitan region showed an increase of 8 percent in the number of short-term beds during 1960-65, and of 15 percent between 1965 and 1970. The most remarkable change occurred in the Long Island region between 1960 and 1965, with an increase of 50 percent, while the increase between 1965 and 1970 was only 6 percent, as seen in Table 5.6. (The late 1950s and early 1960s were a time of marked population growth in the Long Island region.)

TABLE 5.6

Number of Beds in General Care Facilities, by Region, 1960-70

| | | | | Percent Change | |
Region	1960	1965	1970	1960-65	1965-70
Rochester	4,086	4,206	4,391	+4	+3
Northern metropolitan	5,824	6,279	7,220	+8	+15
New York City	37,872	38,351	39,373	+1	+3
Long Island	4,254	6,394	6.803	+50	+6
Total	52,036	55,230	57,787	+6	+5

Source: Compiled by the author.

Analysis of Observed Change in Short-Term Beds, 1960-70

In order to determine whether changes in the number of short-term general care beds during the years prior to enactment of the certificate of need legislation were significantly different from those changes observed after implementation, an analysis was carried out by county and region.

In the following analysis, the null hypothesis was that there was no difference in the mean number of general care beds before and after the certificate of need legislation. It was tested by using a paired-means t-test procedure. The study counties served as the related samples, differences between 1960 and 1965 being compared with changes observed between 1965 and 1970. The standard errors of the differences between these paired samples were estimated during each time period.

The first test of significance was applied to all study counties with respect to short-term beds. The average difference between the number avilable in 1960 as compared to 1965 (an increase of 132 beds) was not significant ($.10 > p > .05$), but the result may be viewed as suggestive.

The test was repeated in order to examine differences in the number of short-term beds in the study counties between 1965 and 1970. There was a positive average difference of 103 beds which was found to be statistically significant ($.01 > p > .001$). This may be seen in Table 5.7. For a discussion of these outcomes see Chapter 8.

The range in the number of short-term general care beds in the study counties is very wide, as might be expected based on the probit

TABLE 5. 7

Observed Difference in the Number of Short-Term Hospital Beds,
by County, 1960-70

County	1960	1965	1970	1960-65	1965-70
Allegany	120	145	176	+25	+31
Chemung	455	518	518	+63	0
Livingston	72	60	60	-12	0
Monroe	2,078	2,095	2,225	+17	+160
Ontario	449	398	364	-51	-34
Orleans	111	118	118	+7	0
Schuyler	52	52	54	0	+2
Seneca	109	120	120	+11	0
Steuben	422	399	428	-23	+29
Wayne	155	211	204	+56	-7
Yates	63	94	94	+31	0
Dutchess	568	570	773	+2	+203
Orange	762	862	932	+100	+70
Putnam	63	138	184	+75	+46
Rockland	556	514	754	-42	+240
Sullivan	247	291	308	+44	+17
Ulster	291	425	550	+134	+125
Westchester	3,237	3,479	3,719	+242	+240
Bronx	4,773	5,480	5,858	+707	+378
Kings	10,131	9,768	10,329	-363	+561
New York	17,048	16,552	16,400	-496	-152
Queens	5,145	5,764	5,893	+619	+131
Richmond	775	787	893	+12	+106
Nassau	2,793	4,074	4,159	+1,281	+85
Suffolk	1,461	2,320	2,644	+859	+324

$$\bar{D} = 132 \qquad \bar{D} = 103$$

$$S_{\bar{D}} = 74 \qquad S_{\bar{D}} = 31$$

$$t_{24} = 1.78 \qquad t_{24} = 3$$

$$.10 > p > .05 \qquad .01 > p > .001$$

Note: In Tables 5.7-5.12 and 5.19-5.24, $\bar{D}$ = average difference; $S_{\bar{D}}$ = standard error of the difference; t_{df} = ratio of the difference taken at the appropriate level of degrees of freedom; and p = probability associated with the ratio. Significance is felt to be present when $p \leq .05$.

Source: Compiled by the author.

analysis described in Chapter 4.* It may be recalled that the counties can be divided into two distinct groups with respect to size of population, and that eight of the study counties were among the ten most populated in the state. It seemed reasonable, therefore, to divide the study counties into two groups, based on the bimodal nature of the size distribution. It should be noted too that the eight most populated counties each had 1,400 or more short-term beds in 1960 and 2,000 or more after 1965.

Once the counties were grouped according to size, the test was repeated, showing the following with respect to short-term beds.

There was a positive but nonsignificant difference between the 1960 and 1965 means for the large counties ($\bar{D}$ = 358, .20 > p > .10). (A positive difference meant that the change was an increase during the interval; a negative difference meant that a decrease occurred.) However, the changes between 1965 and 1970 showed a positive difference of 217 beds which was statistically significant (.05 > p > .02), as seen in Table 5.8. For an explanation of these changes, refer to Chapter 8.

TABLE 5.8

Observed Difference in the Number of Short-Term
Beds in Large Counties, 1960-70

County	1960	1965	1970	1960-65	1965-70
Monroe	2,078	2,095	2,255	+17	+160
Westchester	3,237	3,479	3,719	+242	+240
Bronx	4,773	5,480	5,858	+707	+378
Kings	10,131	9,768	10,329	-363	+561
New York	17,048	16,552	16,400	-496	-152
Queens	5,145	5,764	5,893	+619	+131
Nassau	2,793	4,074	4,159	+1,281	+85
Suffolk	1,461	2,320	2,644	+859	+324

$$\bar{D} = 358 \qquad \bar{D} = 217$$
$$S_{\bar{D}} = 253 \qquad S_{\bar{D}} = 7$$
$$t_7 = 1.41 \qquad t_7 = 2.86$$
$$.20 > p > .10 \qquad .05 > p > .02$$

*Where a linear relationship is assumed to exist between two variables, such as total beds (y) and county population (x), a least-squares line may be generated using the model $y = bx + k$, where b is the slope of the line and k is a constant. To test this hypothesis we set $k = 0$. Thus, we can test the linearity in the hypothesized relationship.

TABLE 5.9

Observed Difference in the Number of Short-Term Beds
in Small Counties, 1960-70

County	1960	1965	1970	1960-65	1965-70
Allegany	120	145	176	+24	+31
Chemung	455	518	518	+63	0
Livingston	72	60	60	-12	0
Ontario	449	398	364	-51	-34
Orleans	111	118	118	+7	0
Schuyler	52	52	54	0	+2
Seneca	109	120	120	+11	0
Steuben	422	399	428	-23	+29
Wayne	155	211	204	+56	-7
Yates	63	94	94	+31	0
Dutchess	568	570	773	+2	+203
Orange	762	862	932	+100	+70
Putnam	63	138	184	+75	+46
Rockland	556	514	754	-42	+240
Sullivan	247	291	308	+44	+17
Ulster	291	425	550	+134	+125
Richmond	775	787	893	+12	+106
				$\bar{D} = 25$	$\bar{D} = 49$
				$S_{\bar{D}} = 12$	$S_{\bar{D}} = 18$
				$t = 2.14$	$t = 2.65$
				$.05 > p > .02$	$.02 > p > .01$

Source: Compiled by the author.

In the less populated counties there was a significant and positive difference between 1960 and 1965 (25 beds) as well as between 1965 and 1970 (49 beds), ($.05 > p > .02$ and $.02 > p > .01$, respectively). Table 5.9 illustrates these differences.

Regional Differences

In order to examine observed changes before and after the certification of need program in each of the four planning areas, a regional analysis was carried out. The following was found with respect to short-term beds. In the Rochester region, the difference between the means in 1960 and 1965 was positive (11 beds) but nonsignificant (.30 > p > .20). The results were almost identical for the second study period, 1965 to 1970. The difference was positive (16 beds) but, again, nonsignificant (.30 > p > .20), as seen in Table 5.10.

In New York City the difference between the 1960 and 1965 means was positive (96 beds) but nonsignificant (.80 > p > .70), and positive (185 beds) for the 1965 and 1970 mean, but, once again, nonsignificant (.30 > p > .20). (See Table 5.11.)

TABLE 5.10

Observed Difference in the Number of Short-Term
Beds in the Rochester Region, 1960-70

County	1960	1965	1970	1960-65	1965-70
Allegany	120	145	176	+25	+31
Chemung	455	518	518	+63	0
Livingston	72	60	60	-12	0
Monroe	2,078	2,095	2,255	+17	+160
Ontario	449	398	361	-51	-34
Orleans	111	118	118	+8	0
Schuyler	52	52	54	0	+2
Seneca	109	120	120	+11	0
Steuben	422	399	428	-23	+29
Wayne	144	211	204	+56	-7
Yates	63	94	94	+31	0

$\bar{D} = 11$ $\bar{D} = 16$

$S_{\bar{D}}$ 10 $S_{\bar{D}} = 15$

$t = 1.14$ $t = 1.10$

.20 > p > .10   .20 > p > .10

Source: Compiled by the author.

When the counties in the northern metropolitan and Long Island regions were examined, it was found that there was a positive average difference of 299 beds between 1960 and 1965 which was suggestive $(.10 > p > .05)$, while the observed changes between the means of 1965 and 1970 were both positive (151 beds) and statistically significant $(.01 > p > .001)$, as seen in Table 5.12.

TABLE 5.11

Observed Difference in the Number of Short-Term Beds
In New York City, 1960-70

County	1960	1965	1970	1960-65	1965-70
Bronx	4,773	5,480	5,858	+707	+378
Kings	10,131	9,768	10,329	-363	+561
New York	17,048	16,552	16,400	-496	-152
Queens	5,145	5,764	5,893	+619	+131
Richmond	775	787	893	+12	+106
				$\bar{D} = 96$	$\bar{D} = 20.5$
				$S_{\bar{D}} = 247$	$S_{\bar{D}} = 122$
				$t_4 = .38$	$t_4 = 1.67$
				$.80 > p > .70$	$.30 > p > .20$

Source: Compiled by the author.

TABLE 5.12

Observed Difference in the Number of Short-Term Beds,
Northern Metropolitan and Long Island Regions, 1960-70

County	1960	1965	1970	1960-65	1965-70
Dutchess	568	570	773	+2	+203
Orange	762	862	932	+100	+70
Putnam	63	138	184	+75	+46
Rockland	556	514	754	-42	+240
Sullivan	247	291	308	+44	+17
Ulster	291	425	550	+134	+125
Westchester	3,237	3,479	3,719	+242	+240
Nassau	2,793	4,074	4,159	+1,281	+85
Suffolk	1,461	2,320	2,644	+859	+324
				$\bar{D} = 299$	$\bar{D} = 151$
				$S_{\bar{D}} = 152$	$S_{\bar{D}} = 36$
				$t_8 = 1.97$	$t_8 = 4.21$
				$.05 > p > .02$	$.01 > p > .001$

Source: Compiled by the author.

OBSERVED CHANGE IN LONG-TERM CARE FACILITIES

The trends with respect to long-term care facilities were similar to those observed for short-term hospital units, but there were some notable differences. * In three of the four study regions, there were fewer units for long-term care in 1970 than there were in 1960. In the Long Island region there was an increase from 60 to 67 units between 1960 and 1965 and a decrease to 64 units by 1970. This can be seen in Table 5.13.

In two of the regions under study, Rochester and northern metropolitan, there were slight changes between 1960 and 1965, before enactment of the certification of need program, while each of these

*"Long-term care facilities," for purposes of this research, means nursing homes and chronic care hospitals excluding tuberculosis hospitals, state mental hospitals, diagnostic, rehabilitation, and public heal centers.

TABLE 5.13

Number of Facilities for Long-Term Care, by Region, 1960-70

Region	1960	1965	1970
Rochester	92	91	80
Northern metropolitan	144	135	98
New York City	194	168	180
Long Island	60	67	64

Source: Compiled by the author.

TABLE 5.14

Average Size of Long-Term Care Units, by Region, 1960-70

Region	Average No. of Beds per Unit		
	1960	1965	1970
Rochester	35	47	69
Northern metropolitan	39	46	77
New York City	104	123	156
Long Island	45	65	103

Source: Compiled by the author.

regions showed a substantial decrease after implementation (-12 percent and -28 percent respectively).

In New York City there was a decrease of 26 units (-13 percent) in the number of long-term care units between 1960 and 1965 but an increase of 12 (+7 percent) between 1965 and 1970.

A positive change in the average size of long-term care units in the study regions was evident between 1960 and 1965, but this trend seemed to accelerate between 1965 and 1970, as seen in Table 5.14.

In 1960 there were 171 long-term care units containing fewer than 25 beds. (Table 5.15 shows the cumulative number and percent of long-term care beds by region and size of unit.) By 1965 that number dropped to 105 and by 1970 there were 56 long-term care units of fewer than 25 beds. Of special interest are the changes in the proportion of long-term care units represented by these small under-25-bed units. Here, too, the trend is continuous and observable both before and after implementation of the program under study and is evident in all

TABLE 5.15

Long-Term Care Facilities, by Size of Unit and Region, 1960-70

Region	1960 Cumulative Percent	No.	1965 Cumulative Percent	No.	1970 Cumulative Percent	No.
Rochester, Total	100	92	100	91	100	80
Under 25 beds	51	47	32	29	20	16
25-49	89	82	82	75	61	49
50-99	98	90	91	83	80	64
100-199	99	91	98	89	94	75
200+	100	92	100	91	100	80
Northern metropolitan, Total	100	144	100	135	100	97
Under 25 beds	44	64	33	44	22	21
25-49	75	108	70	95	44	43
50-99	94	135	93	126	73	71
100-199	99	142	99	133	94	91
200+	100	144	100	135	100	97
New York City, Total	100	194	100	168	100	179
Under 25 beds	23	44	13	22	7	12
25-49	47	92	33	56	27	49
50-99	74	143	61	102	47	84
100-199	89	173	86	145	69	124
200+	100	194	100	168	100	179
Long Island, Total	100	60	100	66	100	64
Under 25 beds	27	16	16	10	11	7
25-49	77	46	65	43	36	23
50-99	93	56	85	56	56	36
100-199	98	59	98	65	89	57
200+	100	60	100	66	100	64

Source: Compiled by the author.

four study regions. For instance, in the Rochester region, more than half (51 percent) of the long-term care units in existence or planned in 1960 contained fewer than 25 beds. This compared with 32 percent in 1965 and 20 percent in 1970.

In the northern metropolitan region that proportion decreased from 44 percent in 1960 to 33 percent in 1965 and fell to 22 percent by 1970, while New York City showed a reduction from 23 percent in 1960 to 13 percent in 1965, down to 7 percent by 1970.

Long Island revealed similar results with a reduction from 27 percent to 16 percent between 1960 and 1965 and from 16 percent to 11 percent between 1965 and 1970. (Table 5.15 shows changes in the distribution of long-term care facilities by size of unit and by region.)

On the other hand, the trend toward larger chronic care and nursing home type facilities was evident both before and after the certification of need program, but the increase was far more dramatic between 1965 and 1970 than it was between 1960 and 1965. For instance, in 1960 there were 25 units for long-term care in facilities of 200 beds or more while that number increased to 28 by 1965 and 73 by 1970.

Differences observed during the study period with respect to type of control of long-term care facilities were similar to those observed for general care facilities, as seen in Table 5.16.

In the Rochester region, 79 percent of long-term care units were in facilities under proprietary auspices in 1960. By 1965, proprietary long-term care units represented 72 percent of the total and by 1970, only 60 percent. The proportion represented by county or local government varied little during the years under study and this was true in all four regions. The proportion of voluntary long-term care units in the Rochester area represented 13 percent in 1960, 18 percent in 1965, and 30 percent by 1970.

In the other three regions, however, there were the following changes in the proportion represented by voluntary and proprietary units. In the northern metropolitan area 26 percent of the long-term units were operated under voluntary auspices in 1960 and 1965, but by 1970 that proportion fell to 21 percent. Proprietary long-term care units represented 68 percent of all such units in 1960 in that region. By 1965, proprietary facilities for long-term care represented 66 percent of the total and by 1970 they represented 69 percent.

Between 1960 and 1965, New York City experienced an increase in the proportion represented by voluntary units from 34 percent to 39 percent and an associated decrease in the proportion represented by proprietary units (from 62 percent down to 55 percent). The reverse was true for 1965-70. During that time period, New York City showed a decrease in the percent of all long-term care units under voluntary ownership and an increase in the proportion represented by those under proprietary control.

In the Long Island region there was a small increase in the percent of all units operated under voluntary auspices (up from 10 percent

TABLE 5.16

Percent Distribution of Long-Term Care Units,
by Region and by Auspices, 1960-70

	Rochester	Northern Metropolitan	New York City	Long Island
1960				
Voluntary	13	26	34	10
Local Government	8	6	4	3
Proprietary	79	68	62	87
1965				
Voluntary	18	26	39	12
Local Government	10	8	6	3
Proprietary	72	66	55	85
1970				
Voluntary	30	21	34	13
Local Government	10	9	6	3
Proprietary	60	69	60	84

Source: Compiled by the author.

to 12 percent between 1960 and 1965 and up to 13 percent by 1970).
A concurrent decrease was observed in the proportion represented by
proprietary units, as shown in Table 5.16.

In 1960, in three of the four study regions, 65 percent or more of
the long-term care beds were nonconforming, that is, they were in
nonfire-resistive structures, and nearly all of these were nursing
homes (see Table 5.17). All 25 study counties contained such nonconforming units at the beginning of the study period. By 1965, only
one of the 25 counties under study had achieved 100 percent conformance of long-term care units, but by 1970 five of these counties
fit that description. An overall reduction in nonconforming long-term
care units was evident between 1960 and 1965 and in all four study
regions, but that reduction was more dramatic between 1965 and 1970.
For example, in Rochester, there were 2,246 nonconforming long-term
care units, representing 69 percent of the total in 1960. By 1965 that
number dropped to 1,819 or 47 percent of the total and fell to 913 or
16 percent of the total by 1970.

A similar trend was observed in the northern metropolitan and
Long Island regions where the number and percent in 1960 were 3,708
or 65 percent and 1,881 or 70 percent in 1960, respectively. By 1965,
the number of nonconforming units in the northern metropolitan region

TABLE 5.17

Long-Term Care Beds in Nonfire-Resistive Structures,
by Region, 1960-70

	1960		1965		1970	
	No.	Percent of Total	No.	Percent of Total	No.	Percent of Total
Rochester	2,246	69	1,819	42	913	16
Northern metropolitan	3,708	65	3,244	52	1,351	18
New York City	3,187	16	2,494	12	2,189	8
Long Island	1,881	70	1,968	46	693	10

Source: Compiled by the author.

was down to 3,244 or 52 percent, and by 1970 there were 1,351 beds
in nonfire-resistive structures, representing 18 percent of the total.
Long Island experienced a similar reduction, down to 1,968 or 46 percent by 1965 (from 1,881 or 70 percent in 1960) and down to 693 or
10 percent by 1970.

Analysis of Observed Change in Long-Term Care Beds, 1960-70

In 1960, there were in existence and approved for construction an
estimated 31,753 beds in long-term care facilities in the four regions
under study. By 1965, that number reached 35,323, and by 1970 there
were 47,594 long-term beds in existence or planned. (Table 5.18
shows the total number of beds in long-term care facilities by region.)
There was great variation among the four study regions during
each of the two time segments which constitute the study period. However, as may be seen from Table 5.18, the four regions may be
classified into two groups. For example, in New York City and the
northern metropolitan region, the increases were 2 percent and 9 percent
between 1960 and 1965, but 36 percent and 21 percent respectively
between 1965 and 1970. In the Rochester area the increase was 32
percent between 1960 and 1965 and 29 percent in the period 1965-70,
while the Long Island region experienced a 59 percent increase from
1960 to 1965 and a 55 percent increase between 1965 and 1970.
When the test of significance was applied to all study counties
it was found that there was a positive difference of 143 beds between
the 1960 and 1965 means which was statistically significant ($.05 > p
> .02$). Between 1965 and 1970 the positive difference jumped to 491

beds, which was highly significant (.01 > p > .001). Table 5.19 shows the observed difference in the number of long-term care beds by county.

The difference observed in the most populated counties between 1960 and 1965 was positive (317 beds) but nonsignificant (.20 > p > .10). During the period 1965 to 1970 there was an average increase of 1,177 beds in these counties, which was significant (.01 > p > .001). (See Table 5.20.)

Changes observed in the small, less populated counties were positive during both time periods. The difference was found to be statistically significant between 1960 and 1965 (.02 > p > .01) but nonsignificant between 1965 and 1970 (.20 > p >.10). Table 5.21 shows the changes observed in the small counties between 1960 and 1970.

Regional Differences

When the data were grouped according to region the following results were obtained. In the Rochester region, the difference in the number of long-term care beds between 1960 and 1965 was positive (94 beds) but nonsignificant (.20 > p > .10). Again, as in the case of short-term bed growth during the study period, the results for the years 1965 to 1970 were almost identical in this region. The difference was positive (114 beds) but nonsignificant (.30 > p > .20). This is shown in Table 5.22.

Most remarkable, perhaps, are the changes observed in New York City. Between 1960 and 1965 there was an increase of only 90 beds,

TABLE 5.18

Total Number of Beds in Long-Term Care
Facilities, by Region, 1960-70

Region	1960	1965	1970	Percent Change	
				1960-65	1965-70
Rochester	3,253	4,285	5,541	+32	+29
Northern metropolitan	5,683	6,185	7,489	+9	+21
New York City	20,136	20,585	27,947	+2	+36
Long Island	2,681	4,268	6,617	+59	+55
Total	31,753	35,323	47,594	+11	+35

Source: Compiled by the author.

TABLE 5.19

Observed Difference in the Number of Long-Term
Care Beds, by County, 1960-70

County	1960	1965	1970	1960-65	1965-70
Allegany	52	164	176	+112	+12
Chemung	112	214	371	+102	+157
Livingston	109	241	208	+132	-33
Monroe	1,926	2,578	3,549	+652	+971
Ontario	267	294	401	+27	+107
Orleans	235	192	179	-43	-13
Schuyler	25	0	40	-25	+40
Seneca	94	86	33	-8	-53
Steuben	170	223	356	+53	+133
Wayne	210	229	184	+19	-45
Yates	53	64	44	+11	-20
Dutchess	430	476	753	+46	+277
Orange	407	484	623	+77	+139
Putnam	51	47	174	-4	+127
Rockland	467	631	838	+164	+207
Sullivan	145	94	155	-51	+61
Ulster	416	538	462	+122	-76
Westchester	3,767	3,915	4,485	+148	+570
Bronx	4,725	4,565	5,892	-160	+1,327
Kings	5,454	5,567	5,692	+113	+125
New York	7,592	7,182	8,355	-410	+1,173
Queens	1,653	2,255	5,155	+602	+2,900
Richmond	712	1,016	2,853	+304	+1,837
Nassau	1,258	2,557	4,098	+1,299	+1,541
Suffolk	1,423	1,711	2,519	+288	+808

$\bar{D} = 143$ $\bar{D} = 491$

$S_{\bar{D}} = 64$ $S_{\bar{D}} = 150$

$t_{24} = 2.23$ $t_{24} = 3.28$

$.05 > p > .02$ $.01 > p > .001$

Source: Compiled by the author.

TABLE 5.20

Observed Difference in the Number of Long-Term Beds in Large Counties, 1960-70

County	1960	1965	1970	1960-65	1965-70
Monroe	1,926	2,578	3,549	+652	+971
Westchester	3,767	3,915	4,485	+148	+570
Bronx	4,725	4,565	5,892	-160	+1,327
Kings	5,454	5,567	5,692	+113	+125
New York	7,592	7,182	8,355	-410	+1,173
Queens	1,653	2,255	5,155	+602	+2,900
Nassau	1,258	2,557	4,098	+1,299	+1,541
Suffolk	1,423	1,711	2,519	+288	+808
				$\bar{D} = 317$	$\bar{D} = 1,177$
				$S_{\bar{D}} = 188$	$S_{\bar{D}} = 289$
				$t_7 = 1.68$	$t_7 = 4.07$
				$.20 > p > .10$	$.01 > p > .001$

Source: Compiled by the author.

71

TABLE 5. 21

Observed Difference in the Number of Long-Term Care
Beds in Small Counties, 1960-70

County	1960	1965	1970	1960-65	1965-70
Allegany	52	164	176	+112	+12
Chemung	112	214	371	+102	+157
Livingston	109	241	208	+132	-33
Ontario	267	294	401	+27	+107
Orleans	235	192	179	-43	-13
Schuyler	25	0	40	-25	+40
Seneca	94	86	33	-8	-53
Steuben	170	223	356	+53	+133
Wayne	210	229	184	+19	-45
Yates	53	64	44	+11	-20
Dutchess	430	476	753	+46	+277
Orange	407	484	623	+77	+139
Putnam	51	47	174	-4	+127
Rockland	467	631	838	+164	+207
Sullivan	145	94	155	-51	+61
Ulster	416	538	462	+122	-76
Richmond	712	1,016	2,853	+304	+1,837

$$\bar{D} = 61 \qquad \bar{D} = 168$$
$$S_{\bar{D}} = 22 \qquad S_{\bar{D}} = 107$$
$$t_{16} = 2.81 \qquad t_{16} = 1.57$$
$$.05 > p > .02 \quad .20 > p > .10$$

Source: Compiled by the author.

TABLE 5.22

Observed Difference in the Number of Long-Term Beds in the Rochester Region, 1960-70

County	1960	1965	1970	1960-65	1965-70
Allegany	52	164	176	+112	+12
Chemung	112	214	371	+102	+157
Livingston	109	241	208	+132	+33
Monroe	1,926	2,578	3,549	+652	+971
Ontario	267	294	401	+27	+107
Orleans	235	192	179	-43	-13
Schuyler	25	0	40	-25	+40
Seneca	94	86	33	-8	-53
Steuben	170	223	356	+53	+133
Wayne	210	229	184	+19	-45
Yates	53	64	44	+11	-20

$\bar{D} = 94$ $\bar{D} = 114$

$S_{\bar{D}} = 58$ $S_{\bar{D}} = 89$

$t_{10} = 1.61$ $t_{10} = 1.29$

$.20 > p > .10$ $.30 > p > .20$

Source: Compiled by the author.

73

TABLE 5.23

Observed Difference in the Number of Long-Term Beds, New York City, 1960-70

County	1960	1965	1970	1960-65	1965-70
Bronx	4,725	4,565	5,892	-160	+1,327
Kings	5,454	5,567	5,692	+113	+125
New York	7,592	7,182	8,355	-410	+1,173
Queens	1,653	2,255	5,155	+602	+2,900
Richmond	712	1,016	2,853	+304	+1,837

$\bar{D} = 90$ $\bar{D} = 1,472$

$S_{\bar{D}} = 176$ $S_{\bar{D}} = 453$

$t_4 = .51$ $t_4 = 3.25$

$.70 > p > .60$ $.05 > p > .02$

Source: Compiled by the author.

TABLE 5. 24

Observed Difference in the Number of Long-Term Beds
in Northern Metropolitan and Long Island, 1960-70

County	1960	1965	1970	1960-65	1965-70
Dutchess	430	476	753	+46	+277
Orange	407	484	623	+77	+139
Putnam	51	47	174	-4	+127
Rockland	467	631	838	+164	+207
Sullivan	145	94	155	-51	+61
Ulster	416	538	462	+122	-76
Westchester	3, 767	3, 915	4, 485	+148	+570
Nassau	1, 258	2, 557	4, 098	+1, 299	+1, 541
Suffolk	1, 423	1, 711	2, 519	+288	+808

$\bar{D} = 232$ $\bar{D} = 406$

$S_{\bar{D}} = 137$ $S_{\bar{D}} = 168$

$t_8 = 1.69$ $t_8 = 2.42$

$.20 > p > .10$ $.05 > p > .02$

Source: Compiled by the author.

which was nonsignificant ($p > .60$). However, between 1965 and 1970 there was a statistically significant increase of 1, 472 beds ($.05 > p > .02$). Positive and negative changes in New York City are shown for 1960-70 by county in Table 5. 23.

The northern metropolitan and Long Island regions experienced an average positive change of 232 long-term care beds between 1960 and 1965, which was found to be nonsignificant ($.20 > p > .10$). Between 1965 and 1970 there was an average increase of 406 beds in these regions, which was statistically significant ($.05 > p > .02$), as shown in Table 5. 24.

6

**ANALYTICAL MODEL
FOR EVALUATION OF
OBSERVED CHANGE**

In the previous chapter, changes observed with respect to general care and long-term care facilities were described for the period before and after passage of the certificate of need laws, and county and regional analyses were carried out.

In order to better explain and interpret these observed changes, further analysis seemed necessary. In seeking to evaluate the impact of the program on health facility planning outcomes, it became apparent that an analysis of the relationships between the dependent variables, defined for purposes of this research as changes in the number of general care and long-term care beds, and a logical set of independent variables, defined below, would be needed.

A multiple regression analysis was the method selected because it allowed the researcher to study relationships between the two dependent variables and a constellation of independent variables.

The purpose of this type of analysis is well described by N. R. Draper and H. Smith as a "technique of extracting, from masses of data . . . the main features of the relationships hidden or implied in the tabulated figures."[1]

There is a basic assumption that a linear relationship exists between the dependent variables and the set of independent variables specified. (See Appendix A for description of all variables, dependent and independent.) The regression analysis takes into account inter-relationships among the independent variables and relates changes in the dependent variables to differences among the independent variables in order to help predict and explain the variance observed among the study units, in this case, counties.

The regression equation used for this analysis is

$$Y = b_1 x_1 + b_2 x_2 + \ldots + b_n x_n + c + r$$

where Y = change in the number of beds in the two five-year intervals (general care or long-term care), the X's are the independent variables specified, the b's are the regression coefficients, c is a constant, and r is the residual.

SPECIFICATION OF INDEPENDENT VARIABLES

The criteria for selection of the independent variables used in this analytical model included (1) their use in other empirical studies, (2) the author's understanding of the intent of the certification of need program, and (3) the author's expectations as to factors which might logically be associated with changes in the dependent variables over time.

These factors or independent variables can be classified into two main categories. The first can be described as demographic characteristics of the counties. They include (1) population variables such as size of population, change in population size for each time period, population 65 years and over, and change in the population 65 and over for the same two time periods; (2) median family income; (3) total number of nonfederal physicians; and (4) total number of interns and residents in graduate medical education programs (referred to in the remainder of this report as house staff).

The second category contains variables which are thought to reflect selected planning goals of the state Department of Health during the study period. They include (1) estimated percent of need met for general care and long-term care beds, and (2) number of such nonconforming beds in each county.

In the description which follows, the relationships expected between these independent variables and the outcome variables will be described. The actual relationships found through the analysis will be presented in the next chapter.

POPULATION VARIABLES

Size of Population

It seems especially important to include size of the county population as an independent variable in this analysis for the following reasons. First, it has been observed earlier in this report that the counties represent two distinct groupings in terms of population size. The results of the probit analysis (Chapter 4) revealed that there are eight large counties which characterize one universe, while the remaining 17 smaller counties represent another. It is expected that changes in the dependent variables may show a different relationship to this variable in the large counties than in the small ones.

A second reason for inclusion of size of population is the assumption that changes in the number of general care and long-term care beds will be related to size of county population whether or not a need exists for such changes.

It has been noted by other researchers that existing institutions tend to expand, often as a matter of survival.[2] Some have called this phenomenon the "institutional imperative." It will be of great interest, for purposes of this analysis, to observe the relationship therefore, between change in the number of beds and size of population, especially in those counties which experienced an outmigration of population during the study period.

It may be argued that patients are now more mobile than ever before and that such outmigration of population does not necessarily influence their utilization patterns. Despite the fact that certain urban referral centers service a large population from areas well beyond the county where the facility is located, the evidence seems to point to the fact that patients do use facilities near their places of residence if such facilities are available. Further, a goal of many communities is self-sufficiency in terms of availability of general care and long-term care beds. On the other side is the deep concern that unnecessary expansionism leads to unnecessary utilization. The importance of examining and analyzing the influence of population size on changes in inpatient bed capacity before and after introduction of the cerificate of need laws seems to be reinforced by this kind of concern among planners and others.

Change in Population Size

Change in the size of the population is expected to be positively correlated with changes in the number of health care facilities serving it. During the study period, planning units, at the local and state level in New York State (and elsewhere) had been required to take into account anticipated changes in the size of the population of each county served in the development of their annual state plans. In these plans five-year projection figures were used as a basis for estimating need and for assigning priorities for allocation of Hill-Burton construction funds. It will thus be important, in the evaluation of the certificate of need program, to observe the relationships, before and after implementation, between population change and change in bed capacity in the study counties.

Population 65 and Over

In general, the population 65 years of age and older is known to utilize general care hospitals and long-term care facilities more than other groups because they characteristically suffer from more chronic diseases than do others. The selection of population 65 years and older and change in the size of this age group as independent variables is based on the assumption that a high proportion of or major change in the size of the aged population will be closely correlated with change in short-term and long-term care beds within the study counties.

Total Number of Nonfederal Physicians

The influence of the physician on the use of health care facilities is well documented. Gerald Rosenthal points out, in his classic study of demand for hospital facilities, that "once the consumer has entered the [health care] market by seeing a physician, many of the decisions relating to the actual type and amounts of medical care consumed are made by the physician rather than by the consumer himself."[3] Rosenthal goes on, "while many other aspects of the organization of medical care affect the demand for general hospital facilities, there seems to be a consensus that the role of the physician is of primary importance."[4]

Since physicians' behavior has such a direct influence on the demand for inpatient facilities, it seemed reasonable for the analysis to include as an independent variable the total number of nonfederal physicians in each of the 25 study counties.

House Staff

The number of doctors in graduate medical education programs (internships and residencies) has been selected as an independent variable because the author believes there will be a significant relationship between this variable and the outcome variables, especially with respect to observed change in the number of general care beds. This is thought to be the case because of the heavy emphasis, in most such training programs, on care of the acutely ill patient.

It is hypothesized therefore that the direction of the relationship between number of house staff and change in the number of general care beds will be positive. On the other hand, it is not clear what the relationship between house staff and change in long-term care beds might be, if any, and therefore no prediction will be made here regarding this relationship.

Median Family Income

Inclusion of median family income is thought to be important because it embodies a measure of the income distribution within the study counties. It is expected that this independent variable will be correlated with changes in both general care and long-term care beds during the study period.

PLANNING VARIABLES

Estimated Percent of Need Met for General Care Beds

Perhaps the most critical independent variable to be included in this analytical model is the estimated percent of need met for general care beds. This is thought to be so because the certificate of need program was aimed, in large part, at a rational distribution of such beds, based on demonstrated need. It will be recalled that the Folsom Committee found that too many general care beds existed in some areas of the state while other areas had too few. In the evaluation of the impact of the program under study, a careful examination of the relationship between increased bed capacity and need met by existing suitable beds during each of the time segments comprising the study period seems essential.

It is expected that the direction of this relationship will be negative. For example, where the estimated percent of need met in a given county was close to 100 percent it would be assumed that there would be little or no change in the number of general care beds during the subsequent five-year period. On the other hand, in counties where the percent of need met was low, it would be expected that change in the number of general care beds would be high. A perfect correlation between change in general care beds and percent of need met would therefore be -1.00, negative because of the expected inverse relationship between the two variables.

It is interesting to note that in both 1960 and 1965, the study counties showed the full range of possibilities, in terms of percent of need met, from the lowest one possible (estimated at 38 percent in 1960 and 00 percent in 1965) to the highest (100 percent in 1960, 112 percent in 1965) with a representative distribution between these extremes.

Estimated Percent of Need Met for Long-Term Care Beds

It is important to include estimated percent of need met for long-term care beds as an independent variable because of the extraordinary need for additional nursing home and chronic care units during the years under study. It can be noted, for example, that 15 of the 25 study counties showed under 50 percent estimated percent of need met in 1960. By 1965, at least ten of the 25 study counties had achieved less than 50 percent of the estimated percent of need met for such beds.

It is expected therefore that change in the number of such beds will be poorly correlated with estimated percent of need met for long-term care beds. This is anticipated because so many counties showed a low estimate of need met for both 1960 and 1965.

Nonconforming General Care and Long-Term Care Beds

Nonconforming general care and long-term care beds are included as independent variables because of the apparent problem in some areas of the state with respect to unsafe, nonfire-resistive structures. It is expected that—where such a problem existed, for instance in the large counties of the state—a positive relationship would be found between nonconforming beds and change in the number of general care and long-term care beds.

In the analysis which follows, there is a description of the overall correlations between each of the two dependent variables and the set of independent variables included in the analysis. Simple correlations are also described in rank order for the two segments of the study period. This is followed by the application of a stepwise regression technique which provides a powerful tool for selecting those independent vailables which contributed most to the analysis.

NOTES

1. N. R. Draper and H. Smith, Applied Regression Analysis (New York: John Wiley and Sons, Inc., 1966), p. 1.

2. For an interesting discussion of the hospital bed population problem, see Frank Bench, "Tomorrow's Hospital Bed Population," Hospital Forum (May 1974): 10-12.

3. Gerald Rosenthal, The Demand for General Care Hospital Facilities (Chicago: American Hospital Association, 1964), p. 7.

4. Ibid., p. 7.

7

**BEFORE-AFTER
CORRELATIONS
WITH PLANNING
AND POPULATION
VARIABLES**

In the preceding chapter, the independent variables which were expected to be closely associated with changes in the number of general care and long-term care beds were described. Following are the results with respect to relationships using the simple correlations and the multiple regression model described in Chapter 6.

GENERAL CARE BEDS

All Study Counties

Before 1965, the highest simple correlation observed between change in the number of general care beds in all 25 study counties and planning and population characteristics was change in the size of the county population ($r = .6964$; $p < .001$). Change in the size of the population 65 and over and median family income were highly correlated with change in the number of general care beds ($r = .5576$ and $r = .5575$, respectively). After 1965, the simple correlations between change in the number of general care beds and these three independent variables were substantially lower. Their rank order dropped from first, second, and third before 1965 to sixth, fifth, and seventh place, respectively, between 1965 and 1970. This can be seen in Table 7.1.

An interesting statistical finding was the negative correlation found between change in general care beds and estimated percent of need met for such beds ($r = -.3051$ before and $r = -.1096$ after 1965). The direction of this relationship is one which was expected. It was anticipated that smaller positive changes would have occurred in counties where a higher estimated percent of the need for general care beds had been achieved than where there was a greater estimated need for additional beds. However, it is interesting to note that the

TABLE 7.1

Simple Correlations in Rank Order, All Study Counties

Changes in General Care Beds Versus:

Variables	1960-65		1965-70		Significance of Change in r
	Rank	r	r	Rank	
Change in population size	1	0.6964[c]	0.4459[a]	6	
Change in population 65+	2	0.5576[b]	0.4647[a]	5	
Median family income	3	0.5575[b]	0.2026	7	
Nonconforming general care beds	4	-0.3819[a]	0.5234[b]	4	b
Estimated percent need met (general care beds)	5	-0.3051	-0.1096	11	
Nonconforming long-term care beds	6	0.2994	0.5972[c]	2	
House staff	7	-0.2027	0.1120	10	
Size of population	8	0.1859	0.6081	1	borderline
Number of physicians	9	-0.1318	0.1146	9	
Population 65+	10	0.0514	0.5245[b]	3	borderline
Estimated percent need met (long-term care beds)	11	-0.0430	-0.1223	8	

[a] .05 > p > .01
[b] .01 > p > .001
[c]   p < .001

df = 23

Source: Compiled by the author.

correlation, while negative for both 1960-65 and 1965-70, was lower after introduction of the certificate of need law than before.

A striking finding is the correlation between change in general care beds and the number of such beds found to be nonconforming. Before 1965 the correlation was negative (r = -.3819), while the reverse was true for the 1965-70 interval (r = .5234), and the change in r between these two time intervals was found to be statistically significant.

No significant association was found between change in the number of general care beds and the remaining variables before 1965, but it should be noted that there was an inverse relationship between such changes and the number of physicians and house staff, as well as for estimated percent of need met for long-term care beds.

After the implementation of the law, the following changes were noted. The highest correlation was found between change in the number of general care beds and the size of the county population (r = .6081). Interestingly, size of population ranked only eighth before 1965 (r = .1859).

There was a positive correlation for the 1965-70 interval between change in general care beds and nonconforming long-term care beds (r = .5972) as well as with population 65 years of age and over (r = .5245), and nonconforming general care beds (r = .5234). However, the association between such changes and median family income, number of physicians, and number of house staff was low, in each case r = .2026 or less, while that association was negative with respect to estimated percent of need met for long-term care beds (r = -.1223).

Large Study Counties

The following was observed when the counties were grouped according to size of population. Changes in the number of general care beds in the large counties for the 1960-65 period were most highly correlated with the number of nonconforming general care beds in these counties, but the association was negative (r = -.7712). There was a strong negative correlation, in addition, between such changes and the estimated percent of need met for general care beds (r = -.7053) as well as with the estimated percent of need met for long-term care beds (r = -.7059). Positive correlations were found between change in general care beds and changes in population, median family income, and change in population 65 and over (r = .6649, r = .6255, and r = .4053, respectively). On the other hand, there was a negative correlation between change in general care beds in these counties and house staff (r = -.6565), population 65 and over (r = -.6303), and size of population (r = -.3823). Table 7.2 describes simple correlations for the eight most populous counties.

After 1965, the independent variables which ranked first, second, and third each showed a negative association to observed change in general care beds. Moreover, the simple correlations between such changes and size of population, nonconforming general care beds, or change in population, while positive, were relatively low (r = .3501, r = .3374, r = .2636, respectively).

The association between change in general care beds and estimated percent of need met for general care beds was negative for both time periods, as might be expected, but was substantially lower for 1965-70 than it was for 1960-65 (r = -.7053 for 1960-65, and r = -.2903 for 1965-70).

No particular association was found between general care bed changes and either population 65 and over or change in population 65 and over for 1965-70 in the large counties.

TABLE 7. 2

Simple Correlations in Rank Order, Eight Large Counties

Changes in General Care Beds Versus:

Variables	1960-65		1965-70		Significance of Change in r
	Rank	r	r	Rank	
Nonconforming general care beds	1	-0.7712[b]	0.3374	5	a
Estimated percent need met (long-term care beds)	2	-0.7059[a]	-0.5438	1	
Estimated percent need met (general care beds)	3	-0.7053[a]	-0.2903	6	
Change in population size	4	-0.6649[a]	0.2636	8	
Number of physicians	5	-0.6565[a]	-0.5234	2	
House staff	6	-0.6303	-0.3545	3	
Median family income	7	0.6255	-0.2392	9	
Population 65+	8	-0.5878	0.1652	10	
Change in population 65+	9	0.4030	0.1144	11	
Size of population	10	-0.3823	0.3501	4	
Nonconforming long-term care beds	11	-0.0625	0.2820	7	

[a] $.05 > p > .01$
[b] $.01 > p > .001$
[c] $p < .001$
df = 6
Source: Compiled by the author.

Small Counties

Tho simple correlations betwoon observed change in the number of general care beds and the variables included in the analysis were low for the period 1960-65 in the smaller counties. That was not the case for the period after 1965. The variables which ranked highest for 1965-70 were population size (r = .8604), change in population size (r = .8529), and house staff (r = .7797). Changes in the number of

TABLE 7. 3

Simple Correlations in Rank Order, 17 Small Counties

Changes in General Care Beds Versus:

Variables	1960-65		1965-70		Significance of Change in r
	Rank	r	r	Rank	
Population 65+	1	0.1921	-0.0007	11	
Estimated percent need met, general care beds	2	-0.1738	-0.2311	9	
Median family income	3	-0.1726	-0.1411	10	
Change in population size	4	-0.1258	0.8529^c	2	c
Size of population	5	0.1102	0.8604^c	1	c
Change in population 65+	6	0.0999	0.4366	8	
Number of physicians	7	-0.0960	0.6912^b	7	a
Nonconforming long-term care beds	8	0.0855	0.7027^c	6	a
House staff	9	-0.0544	0.7797^c	3	b
Nonconforming general care beds	10	0.0520	0.7761^c	4	b
Estimated percent need met, long-term care beds	11	-0.0075	0.7723^c	5	b

a .05 > p > .01
b .01 > p > .001
c p < .001
df = 15
Source: Compiled by the author.

general care beds were also highly correlated with the number of non-conforming general care beds in these counties (r = .7761) as well as with estimated percent of need met for long-term care beds (r = .7723), nonconforming long-term care beds (r = .7027), and the number of physicians (r = .6912). There was a positive correlation between general care bed changes and change in the population 65 and over (r = .4366), but this variable ranked eighth among all the variables included in the analysis.

It is interesting to note that observed change in the number of general care beds was negatively correlated with estimated percent of need met for general care beds during each time period and that the correlation was higher for 1965-70 than it was before 1965 (r = -.1738 and r = -.2311, respectively). Table 7.3 shows the simple correlations for the 17 small counties.

LONG-TERM CARE BEDS

All Study Counties

The simple correlations found between change in the number of long-term care beds and the independent variables used in the analysis were as follows for all study counties (see Table 7.4).

Median family income ranked first before 1965 (r = .7199), while change in population size and change in population 65 and over ranked second and third (r = .5269 and r = .5155, respectively). There was a negative correlation between long-term care bed changes and the number of physicians (r = -.1101), number of house staff (r = -.2893), estimated percent of need met for general care beds (r = -.2447), and nonconforming general care beds (r = -.2341).

The association between change in long-term care beds and nonconforming long-term care beds in each county was positive but low (r = .2755). The same was true of the simple correlations between long-term care bed changes and size of population, population 65 and over, and estimated percent of need met for long-term care beds (r = .2236, r = .0686, r = .0074, respectively).

After 1965, change in long-term care beds was most highly correlated with change in population 65 and over (r = .7767). The remaining independent variables showed the following relationships to change in long-term care beds. Size of population ranked second (r = .6260), while population 65 and over, number of physicians, and change in population size ranked third, fourth and fifth (r = .6204, r = .4704, r = .3740, respectively). None of the remaining variables showed any particular association to change in long-term care beds.

Large Counties

Changes in the number of long-term care beds in the large counties for the period 1960-65 were most highly correlated with median family income (r = .8185) but were negatively correlated with house staff (r = -.7227) and total number of physicians (r = -.5841). Such changes showed an inverse relationship to estimated percent of need met for general care facilities and nonconforming general care beds (r = -.6421

TABLE 7.4

Simple Correlations in Rank Order, All Study Counties

Changes in Long-Term Care Beds Versus:

Variables	1960-65		1965-70		Significance of Change in r
	Rank	r	r	Rank	
Median family income	1	0.7199[c]	0.3622	6	
Change in population size	2	0.5269[b]	0.3740	5	
Change in population 65+	3	0.5155[a]	0.7767[c]	1	
House staff	4	-0.2893	0.3534	8	a
Nonconforming long-term care beds	5	0.2755	0.3337	9	
Estimated percent need met, general care beds	6	-0.2447	-0.0679	11	
Nonconforming general care beds	7	-0.2341	0.3597	7	a
Size of population	8	0.2236	0.6260[c]	2	
Number of physicians	9	-0.1101	0.4704[a]	4	a
Population 65+	10	0.0686	0.6204[c]	3	a
Estimated percent need met, long-term care beds	11	0.0074	0.1625	10	

[a] $.05 > p > .01$

[b] $.01 > p > .001$

[c] $p < .001$

df = 23

Source: Compiled by the author.

and $r = -.5557$, respectively). Population 65 and over was also negatively correlated with changes in long-term beds ($r = -.4954$), while change in population and change in population 65 and over showed a relatively weak but positive association with such changes for that time period ($r = .4364$ and $r = .3709$). Table 7.5 shows the simple correlations, for the large counties, between change in the number of long-term care beds and the set of independent variables used in the analysis.

By 1970, the change in long-term care beds was most highly correlated with change in the population 65 and over (r = .6940). Nonconforming long-term care beds ranked second among all the variables, but it is interesting to note that the direction of this association was negative (r = -.5675). Correlations between changes in long-term care beds and the remaining variables were generally weak but positive, with the exception of house staff, number of physicians, and nonconforming general care beds, where the associations were negative.

TABLE 7.5

Simple Correlations in Rank Order, Eight Large Counties

Changes in Long-Term Care Beds Versus:

Variables	1960-65		1965-70		Significance of Change in r
	Rank	r	r	Rank	
Median family income	1	0.8185[b]	0.1271	7	
House staff	2	-0.7227[a]	-0.1234	8	
Estimated percent of need met, general care beds	3	-0.6421[a]	0.2374	3	
Number of physicians	4	-0.5841	-0.0105	11	
Nonconforming general care beds	5	-0.5557	-0.1182	9	
Population 65+	6	-0.4954	0.1765	4	
Estimated percent need met, long-term care beds	7	-0.4597	0.1755	5	
Change in population	8	0.4364	0.1353	6	
Change in population 65+	9	0.3709	0.6940[a]	1	
Size of population	10	-0.2386	0.0902	10	
Nonconforming long-term care beds	11	-0.0684	-0.5675	2	

[a] .05 > p > .01

[b] .01 > p > .001

[c] p < .001

df = 6

Source: Compiled by the author.

TABLE 7.6

Simple Correlations in Rank Order, 17 Small Counties

Changes in Long-Term Care Beds Versus:

Variables	1960-65		1965-70		Significance of Change in r
	Rank	r	r	Rank	
Size of population	1	0.7042[c]	0.6811[b]	2	
House staff	2	0.7033[c]	0.9073[c]	1	
Change in population 65+	3	0.6824[b]	0.6340[b]	3	
Change in population	4	0.6565[b]	0.6012[b]	6	
Number of physicians	5	0.6447[b]	0.6217[b]	4	
Population 65+	6	0.6004[b]	0.6097[b]	5	
Median family income	7	0.5051[a]	0.4009	8	
Nonconforming long-term care beds	8	0.4416	0.4362	7	
Nonconforming general care beds	9	0.2763	-0.0991	10	
Estimated percent need met, general care beds	10	0.0776	-0.0743	11	
Estimated percent need met, long-term care beds	11	-0.0255	-0.1766	9	

[a] .05 > p > .01

[b] .01 > p > .001

[c] p < .001

df = 15

Source: Compiled by the author.

The directions of these relationships were the same as for the period before 1965, but the correlations were substantially lower for the 1965-70 period than they were for the 1960-65 period.

The most interesting finding is the difference observed in the correlation between changes in long-term care beds and the estimated percent of need met for long-term care beds for the two time periods. It can be noted that the correlation was stronger before introduction of the certificate of need laws than after, and that the correlation was negative for 1960-65 but positive for 1965-70. An interpretation of the probable implications of these findings follows.

Small Counties

Observed change in the number of long-term care beds for 1960-65 in the 17 smaller counties showed a positive and relatively high correlation to the size of the county population (r = .7042), house staff (r = .7033), and change in the population 65 and over (r = .6824). There was a fairly strong positive association, as well, between long-term care bed change and change in population size (r = .6565), number of physicians (r = .6447), and population 65 and over (r = .6004). Table 7.6 shows simple correlations between change in the number of long-term care beds and the independent variables included in the analysis.

By 1970, the independent variable showing the highest simple correlation to long-term care bed changes was house staff (r = .9073). Those ranking second through sixth were: size of population (r = .6811), change in population 65 and over (r = .6340), number of physicians (r = .6217), population 65 and over (r = .6097), and change in population (r = .6012). This cluster of independent variables has significance for the evaluation of the certificate of need program and will be discussed in Chapter 8.

REGIONAL DIFFERENCES

The Rochester Region

An analysis of the relationships between change in the number of general care beds and the set of independent variables chosen showed that in the Rochester planning area there were weak correlations for the period 1960-65. It is interesting to note, however, that a negative relationship was found between general care bed change and estimated percent of need met (r = -.2936), and that this independent variable ranked first for that time period, as shown in Table 7.7.

TABLE 7.7

Simple Correlations in Rank Order, Rochester Region

Change in General Care Beds Vs.:

Variables	1960-65		1965-70		Significance of Change in r
	Rank	r	r	Rank	
Estimated percent need met, general care beds	1	-0.2936	0.1171	10	
Estimated percent need met, long-term care beds	2	0.1936	0.0131	11	
Nonconforming general care beds	3	-0.1689	0.4449	9	
Change in population 65+	4	0.0869	0.8584[c]	7	a
Size of population	5	0.0640	0.9293[c]	4	c
House staff	6	0.0563	0.9404[c]	1	c
Population 65+	7	0.0538	0.9301[c]	3	b
Number of physicians	8	0.0431	0.9315[c]	2	b
Median family income	9	0.0422	0.5640[a]	8	
Change in population	10	0.0346	0.9126[c]	5	b
Nonconforming long-term care beds	11	-0.0113	0.9055[c]	6	b

[a] .05 > p > .01

[b] .01 > p > .001

[c] p < .001

df = 9

Source: Compiled by the author.

After 1965, the simple correlations between change in general care beds and the same independent variables revealed a high positive correlation with seven of the eleven independent variables, suggesting that they are interrelated. In rank order they included: house staff, number of physicians, population 65 and over, size of population, change in population, nonconforming long-term care beds, and change in population 65 and over.

In the case of long-term care beds, the simple correlations were high for both time periods. Although their rank was slightly different, the variables which held first through seventh places were the same for 1960-65 as for 1965-70. Table 7.8 shows that size of population,

number of physicians, change in population 65 and over, population
65 and over, change in population size, house staff, and nonconforming
long-term care beds each showed a strong positive correlation to change
in long-term care beds (r > . 9000 for both time periods). Median family
income ranked eighth before and after 1965 (r = . 7721 and r = . 6897),
while estimated percent of need met showed no particular correlation
to change in general care beds. However, it is worth noting that the
relationship was negative before 1965 but positive after.

TABLE 7. 8

Simple Correlations in Rank Order, Rochester Region

Changes in Long-Term Care Beds Versus:

Variables	1960-65		1965-70		Significance of Change in r
	Rank	r	r	Rank	
Size of population	1	0. 9646[c]	0. 9823[c]	2	
Number of physicians	2	0. 9634[c]	0. 9803[c]	3	
Change in population 65+	3	0. 9633[c]	0. 9206[c]	7	
Population 65+	4	0. 9619[c]	0. 9842[c]	1	
Change in population	5	0. 9567[c]	0. 9579[c]	6	
House staff	6	0. 9557[c]	0. 9682[c]	5	
Nonconforming long-term care beds	7	0. 9357[c]	0. 9722[c]	4	
Median family income	8	0. 7721[b]	0. 6897[b]	8	
Estimated percent need met, long-term care beds	9	0. 3190	0. 0446	10	
Nonconforming general care beds	10	0. 1312	0. 4590	9	
Estimated percent need met, general care beds	11	-0. 0247	0. 0046	11	

[a] . 05 > p > . 01

[b] . 01 > p > . 001

[c] p < . 001

df = 9

Source: Compiled by the author.

TABLE 7.9

Simple Correlations in Rank Order, Northern Metropolitan and Long Island

Changes in General Care Beds Versus:

Variables	1960-65		1965-70		Significance of Change in r
	Rank	r	r	Rank	
Change in population 65+	1	0.9142[c]	0.4485	4	a
Size of population	2	0.8877[c]	0.4145	6	borderline
Estimated percent need met, general care beds	3	-0.8193[b]	-0.3367	7	
Population 65+	4	0.7969[b]	0.4221	5	
Number of physicians	5	0.7652[b]	0.3325	8	
Change in population	6	0.6125[a]	0.7014[a]	1	
Median family income	7	0.5732	0.4580	3	
House staff	8	0.4739	-0.0729	11	
Nonconforming long-term care beds	9	0.3240	0.6645[a]	2	
Estimated percent need met, long-term care beds	10	-0.2623	-0.1322	9	
Nonconforming general care beds	11	-0.1355	-0.0901	10	

[a].05 > p > .01

[b].01 > p > .001

[c]p < .001

df = 7

Source: Compiled by the author.

The Northern Metropolitan and Long Island Regions

In the northern metropolitan and Long Island regions, the change in general care beds was most highly correlated with change in population 65 and over for the period 1960-65 (r = .9142). High positive correlations were also found between change in the number of general care beds and size of population (r = .8877), population 65 and over (r = .7969), and number of physicians (r = .7652), as seen in Table 7.9.

TABLE 7.10

Simple Correlations in Rank Order, Northern Metropolitan and Long Island

Changes in Long-Term Care Beds Versus:

Variables	1960-65		1965-70		Significance of Change in r
	Rank	r	r	Rank	
Size of population	1	0.8617[c]	0.9471[c]	1	
Number of physicians	2	0.7617[b]	0.8895[c]	4	
Change in population 65+	3	0.7546[b]	0.9207[c]	2	
Population 65+	4	0.7139[a]	0.8990[c]	3	
Median family income	5	0.6906[a]	0.7088[a]	6	
Estimated percent need met, general care beds	6	-0.6231[a]	-0.3367	10	
House staff	7	0.5380	0.8663[c]	5	
Change in population	8	0.2682	0.5116	8	
Estimated percent need met, long-term care beds	9	-0.2218	-0.1322	11	
Nonconforming long-term care beds	10	0.1688	0.4996	9	
Nonconforming general care beds	11	-0.1419	0.5586	7	

[a] $.05 > p > .01$

[b] $.01 > p > .001$

[c] $p < .001$

df = 7

Source: Compiled by the author.

By 1970, the strongest simple correlation was found between change in general care beds and change in population ($r = .7014$). Nonconforming long-term care beds ranked second ($r = .6645$), while median family income, population 65 and over, and change in population 65 and over followed ($r = .4580$, $r = .4485$, $r = .4221$, respectively). These three variables showed a much stronger correlation with change in general care beds for the period 1960-65 than they did for the period 1965-70.

The most striking finding was the high negative correlation found between general care bed change and estimated percent of need met before 1965 (r = -.8193). While this relationship remained negative, after 1965 it dropped substantially, to r = -.3367.

The independent variable most highly correlated with change in the number of long-term care beds in the northern metropolitan and Long Island regions was size of population (see Table 7.10). This was true before 1965 (r = .8617) as well as for the interval 1965-70 (r = .9471). The variables ranking second through fifth before 1965 were: number of physicians (r = .7617), change in population 65 and over (r = .7546), population 65 and over (r = .7139), and median family income (r = .6906).

After 1965, change in size of population 65 and over, population 65 and over, number of physicians, and house staff ranked second through fifth, showing high correlations. Change in the number of long-term care beds and estimated percent of need met for such facilities showed that the correlation was higher for 1960-65 than it was for 1965-70 (r = -.2218 as compared to r = -.1322). A negative correlation was also observed between change in the number of long-term care beds and estimated need for general care beds for both time periods and, again, the correlation was stronger before the certificate of need legislation than after (r = -.6231 before 1965, while r = -.3367 for the 1965-70 interval).

In the following chapter, the results of the application of a step-wise multiple regression analysis are described. The method is useful in selecting, one at a time, the independent variables which are the best predictors of observed differences among the study units. In the first step, the variable which best explains the variance is selected, and in each subsequent step another variable is added on the basis of its ability to predict outcomes in conjunction with the first variable, thereby taking into account the interrelationships among the full set of independent variables.

8

BEFORE-AFTER
MULTIPLE REGRESSION
ANALYSES WITH
PLANNING AND
POPULATION VARIABLES

In the following section, the results of ten stepwise multiple regressions are described. In these regression analyses, only those independent variables which were found to make a significant contribution to the prediction equation were included. In the end, nearly all the variables were included in each analysis. The selection of the best predictors was predicated upon whether a new variable, once added, contributed to the significance of the multiple correlation coefficients. In this way, the analyses selected out the fewest independent variables, which, taken together, could best explain the variance among the study counties. This provided a basis for comparing factors predictive of general care and long-term care bed construction between the 1960-65 period (before the certificate of need laws were introduced) and the 1965-70 period, that is, after implementation.

The analyses were designed to evaluate the extent to which county characteristics and planning goals affected observed change in the dependent variables and what possible impact, if any, the timing of the certificate of need program in 1965 may have had on these relationships. Table 8.1 summarizes these findings.

Before the introduction of the certification of need program, four independent variables—change in population size, change in population 65 and over, nonconforming general care beds, and number of physicians—accounted for nearly 80 percent of the variance in general care beds in the 25 study counties (R^2 = .7960).

After implementation, four variables again accounted for over 80 percent of the variance (R^2 = .8282). They were size of population, number of physicians, change in population 65 and over, and nonconforming long-term care beds.

Regarding long-term care beds, before 1965, three variables explained 65 percent of the variance: median income, house staff, and size of population (R^2 = .6594). Between 1965 and 1970, a single

TABLE 8. 1

Planning and Population Variables Accounting for Significant
Proportion of Variance (Derived from Multiple Regression Analyses)

All Study Counties

Variables	General Care Beds 1960-65	1965-70	Long-Term Care Beds 1960-65	1965-70
Population size	—	X	X	--
Change in population size	X	--	--	--
Population 65+	--	—	—	--
Change in population 65+	X	X	--	X
Number of physicians	X	X	—	--
Number of house staff	--	--	X	--
Nonconforming general care beds	X	--	—	---
Nonconforming long-term care beds	--	X	--	—
Estimated percent need met, general care beds	--	—	--	---
Estimated percent need met, long-term care beds	--	—	—	--
Median family income	--	—	X	--
Multiple R^2	0.796	0.828	0.659	0.603

Source: Compiled by the author.

variable, change in the population 65 and over, explained over 60
percent of the variance (R^2 = . 6033).

MULTIPLE CORRELATIONS — BY SIZE OF COUNTY

Before 1965, in the large counties, five variables accounted for
over 99 percent of the variance (R^2 = . 9978): nonconforming general
care beds, estimated percent of need met for long-term care beds,
population 65 and over, number of physicians, and house staff. For
1965-70, again, five variables explained the variance: estimated
percent of need met for long-term care beds, nonconforming general
care beds, number of physicians, house staff, and nonconforming
long-term care beds.

In the smaller counties, before 1965, the four most critical variables associated with change in general care beds were size of

population, number of physicians, change in population 65 and over, and house staff. These variables accounted for 75 percent of the variance (R^2 = .7463). For the 1965-70 interval, change in general care beds in the small counties was most closely associated with the number of physicians. This variable alone accounted for almost 75 percent of the variance (R^2 = .7403) among these counties and was statistically significant.

Before 1965, changes in the number of long-term care beds in the 17 small counties were associated with median family income and with house staff. When the next two independent variables were added into the equation, all four together accounted for over 78 percent of the variance (R^2 = .7855). For 1965-70, the single most important variable associated with change in long-term care beds was house staff, which accounted for over 82 percent of the variance (R^2 = .8231). It was statistically significant.

REGIONAL DIFFERENCES

The Rochester Region

Before certificate of need, the independent variables significantly associated with changes in the number of short-term beds in the Rochester region were estimated percent of need met for general care beds, number of nonconforming general care beds, estimated percent of need met for long-term care beds, population size, and number of nonconforming long-term care beds. These five variables explained 80 percent of the variance (R^2 = .7990). For the 1965-70 interval, the two variables most closely associated with changes in the number of general care beds in the Rochester region were the number of house staff and median family income. These two independent variables accounted for over 96 percent of the variance (R^2 = .9689).

Before 1965, change in the number of long-term care beds in the Rochester region was significantly associated with the size of the population (R^2 = .9457). Between 1965 and 1970, however, population 65 and over became the most critical variable, accounting for over 96 percent of the variance among that region's counties (R^2 = .9686).

The Northern Metropolitan and Long Island Regions

Before 1965, in the northern metropolitan and Long Island regions, the single most important variable associated with change in the number of general care beds was change in the county population 65 and

over, which accounted for 84 percent of the variance ($R^2 = .8357$).
Nonconforming long-term care beds was also statistically significant.
In the northern metropolitan and Long Island regions, changes in
general care beds for the 1965-70 interval were most closely associated
with changes in the size of the population and with the estimated percent of need met for such beds; together these accounted for almost
80 percent of the variance ($R^2 = .7903$).

Before 1965, changes in the number of long-term care beds in the
northern metropolitan and Long Island regions were most closely associated with size of population and population 65 and over. Together
these two variables accounted for over 98 percent of the variance
($R^2 = .9858$). After 1965, population size and nonconforming long-term
care beds were the two best predictors, accounting for 96 percent of
the variance ($R^2 = .9640$).

SUMMARY

The summary relationships between changes in the number of beds
in the 25 study counties and the selected independent variables are
presented in Table 8.2 for 1960-65 and 1965-70. The high multiple
correlation coefficients shown at the bottom of the table indicate that
the variables chosen are strong predictors, accounting as they did for
approximately 90 percent of the variance in both dependent variables
in the two time periods under study. These high correlation coefficients
imply that the variations in growth of both general care and long-term
care beds among the study counties could be explained by county
differences characterized by these independent variables.

General Care Beds

The multiple regression analyses (Table 8.2) indicated that in
1960-65, before the introduction of the certificate of need program, the
best statistical explanation of the variance in change in the number of
general care beds in the study counties was derived from six variables:
population size, change in population size, population 65 and over,
the number of nonconforming general care beds, median family income,
and house staff. Two of the population variables were positively
associated with change in the number of general care beds (population
size and change in population size), as was house staff. However,
changes in the number of general care beds were negatively associated
with the number of nonconforming beds, population 65 and over, and
median family income.

For the 1965-70 interval, the best statistical explanation for such
variance was derived from three variables: number of physicians,

TABLE 8. 2

Standardized Regression Coefficients: Changes in the Number of Beds
in 25 Counties of New York State

Independent Variables	1965 Regression Coefficients		1970 Regression Coefficients	
	GC Beds	LTC Beds	GC Beds	LTC Beds
Constant	557. 8202	-460. 1075	-135. 2759	-1033. 3758
Population size	3. 6416[b]	1. 2635	-0. 3382	-0. 8241
Number of physicians	0. 2453	3. 1623[c]	-1. 8303[b]	-1. 7238[a]
Change in population 65+	0. 3579	-0. 9336[b]	-0. 8651	1. 9205[c]
Nonconforming long-term care beds	-0. 0624	-0. 6225[c]	0. 2718	0. 1289
Population 65+	-3. 7153[c]	0. 7524	2. 1288[a]	-0. 4852
Change in population size	0. 3330[c]	0. 1245	0. 4195[b]	-0. 0418
Median family income	-0. 2235[b]	0. 3294[a]	0. 2203	0. 2976[a]
Estimated percent need met, long-term care beds	-0. 0356	0. 0429	-0. 1087	—
Estimated percent need met, general care beds	-0. 0085	-0. 0644	-0. 0689	—
House staff	0. 8833[a]	-2. 8240[c]	0. 7289	2. 6264[b]
Nonconforming general care beds	-1. 0358[c]	-1. 8137[c]	0. 2238	-0. 2241
R	0. 9811	0. 9354	0. 9541	0. 9201
R^2	0. 9625	0. 8925	0. 9128	0. 8466
df = 13	p < . 001	p < . 001	p < . 001	p < . 001

[a] 0. 05 > p > 0. 01

[b] 0. 01 > p > 0. 001

[c] p < 0. 001

Source: Compiled by the author.

population 65 and over, and change in population size. Three variables appeared to be significantly related to change in general care beds for both the before and after time periods. The association with respect to number of physicians changed from positive before 1965 to negative after, while the reverse was true for population 65 and over. Change in population size was positively associated with change in the dependent variable during both the before and after time intervals.

Long-Term Care Beds

Before 1965, the best statistical explanations of the variance in growth of long-term care facilities were: number of physicians, change in population 65 and over, nonconforming long-term care beds, median family income, house staff, and nonconforming general care beds.

During the 1965-70 time period, the best statistical explanation for variance in the number of long-term care beds in the study counties was derived from four variables: number of physicians, change in population 65 and over, median family income, and house staff. Again, these four variables were significantly related to change in long-term care beds before as well as after 1965. In the case of the number of physicians, that relationship shifted from positive to negative, while the reverse was true for change in population 65 and over.

Median family income was positively associated with such change for both time periods, that is, before introduction of the certificate of need legislation as well as after.

A profound change occurred with respect to postgraduate medical education between 1960-65 and 1965-70. After implementation, there was a change from a negative to a positive association between residency training and increased long-term care bed construction. In both time periods, the association was statistically significant. This change helps underscore the complexity of changes in health care delivery systems such as those intended by this statute.

PART

IV

**SUMMARY AND
CONCLUSIONS**

9

**EVALUATING THE
IMPACT OF
CERTIFICATE OF NEED
LAWS ON HEALTH AND
HOSPITAL FACILITIES
PLANNING OUTCOMES**

In this investigation, evidence has been examined and certain assumptions tested with respect to the impact of certification of need on existing planning functions in one state. The specific questions asked were:

1. What has been the impact of certification of need on the rate and pattern of change in the number of hospital and health care facilities available to the population in selected areas of the state?

2. Has the certification of need program helped planning agencies achieve end results which are closer to desired outcomes than was the case before its implementation?

In order to answer these questions, a study design was used that compared certain observations for the five years before implementation with the five years immediately following. Changes in the number of beds in two types of facilities were described and analyzed: short-term general care, and long-term care.

Also included in the analyses were changes in the number of hospitals and long-term care facilities, their average size, the distribution of these facilities by county, and the number of beds which conformed to U. S. Public Health Service standards for fire-resistiveness.

Statistically significant differences were observed when changes in the number of beds during the first period (before certificate of need) were compared with the number of beds found after implementation.

The univariate analysis of central rates was carried out in three stages:

1. Differences were tested between the average change in the number of beds during each of the two sample time periods, applied to all study counties.

2. Subsequently, counties were grouped according to size ("large" and "small") after it had been established through a probit analysis that the county distribution of population size was bimodal.

3. Finally, the difference in bed capacity observed within four regional planning areas was described and analyzed.

A multiple regression analysis was then performed to determine the beta weights and multiple correlation coefficients for the independent variables. This analysis specifically permitted observation of the relationships between the dependent variables (changes in the number of general care and long-term care beds) and a set of standardized independent variables, including certain population and planning variables (see Chapter 6).

RESUME OF PRINCIPAL FINDINGS

The most noteworthy finding was that, in terms of certain trends, little could be attributed to the introduction in 1965 of the certificate of need legislation for regulating hospital bed expansion. It was observed, for example, that there were generally fewer and larger hospitals in 1970 than in 1960; however, this trend was apparent before 1965 when the law was passed (see Table 5. 2). The proportion of small, theoretically uneconomical short-term general care units (under 50 beds) was reduced during the 1960-70 interval but, here again, the trend was already apparent before 1965 and even seemed to slow down between 1965 and 1970.

The overall increase in the number of short-term hospital beds in all counties studied was smaller in the five-year period after introduction of the certificate of need program than before, a finding which supports the presumption of program success. It should be noted, however, that this result requires qualification, particularly because of the findings from the regression analysis discussed in the sections which follow.

Among the independent variables included in the multiple regression analysis were estimates for each county of the state of need met by existing and planned facilities. These estimates were prepared by state Health Department planning units in conjunction with the planning councils at the local level for counties in their jurisdictions.

At the outset, it was assumed that after the law was implemented the following would occur. (1) Where estimated need was met by existing or planned units, there would be a small increase in the number of additional beds. (2) Where estimated need was sizable, there would be more beds constructed or planned to fulfill such identified needs. (3) Certificate of need would ensure that this would more likely be the case after implementation of the law than before.

Some of the study data seem to indicate that the opposite occurred. In the sections which follow, data supporting and refuting these assumptions are reviewed, discussed, and interpreted. In addition, this research will be examined from the perspective of other studies that have also attempted to evaluate the New York State certificate of need programs.

DISCUSSION OF PRINCIPAL FINDINGS

Some who have recently studied New York State's experience have taken the effective date of the program, February 1, 1966, as the starting point. In one such study, William Leavy compared the health care facilities available in New York State in 1966 with those in 1971, a time period closely approximating the second half of that chosen for this investigation. His findings for that time period were not substantially different from those described in the preceding chapters. However, the conclusions he reached were materially different from those arrived at in this study because of the prelaw (control) data included in our considerations.

As one example, Leavy's report summary states:

The improvements and changes in the quantity and quality of the supply of health facilities . . . over the first five years of the operation of Article 28 is due in large measure to selective approval of the construction of 15,499 totally conforming hospital beds, 35,957 long-term care or nursing home beds. . . .[1]

In another section of his study, Leavy implies that the trend toward fewer but larger and better hospitals across the state was the "result of the effort to discontinue or close uneconomically small, inefficient, duplicative, unsafe, or unnecessary facilities" and that the effort was a result of the certification of need program.

Examining changes during the years 1966 to 1971 exclusively can be somewhat misleading. For example, in three of the four study regions, a trend toward fewer hospitals had already begun before 1965. Long Island, which was experiencing a rapid population growth, showed an increase in the number of hospitals during the period before 1965. In New York City, however, a comparable number of hospitals were eliminated between 1960 and 1965 and between 1965 and 1970, while Rochester, in its general care facilities, showed little change between 1960 and 1965, and no change between 1965 and 1970.

Regarding the trend towards larger units, Leavy wrote that "it is noted that the average size of hospitals and nursing homes has increased markedly, representing fewer but larger and more efficient units."[2]

An examination of the data shows a trend toward larger units between 1960 and 1965 as well as between 1965 and 1970. Not only did that trend exist generally, but in the case of general care units in two of the four study regions the change was as marked (or more marked) before the introduction of the certificate of need laws as after.

Thus, while a post hoc study design such as Leavy's provided interesting findings, the trend he noted had already been established

TABLE 9. 1

Number of General Care Hospitals in All Study Counties,
by Size of Unit, 1960-70

General Care Hospitals	1960		1965		1970	
	No.	Percent of Total	No.	Percent of Total	No.	Percent of Total
Under 50 beds	33	13	18	7	12	5
Under 100 beds	97	39	75	31	56	28

Source: Compiled by the author.

before 1965 and could not be attributed to the certification of need
program (see Tables 9. 1 and 9. 2).

A similar pattern was observed with respect to long-term care
facilities. Small long-term care facilities (under 25 beds) began to
decrease in number before 1965. In fact, the actual proportionate
reduction was greatest between 1960 and 1965. Interestingly, while
the average size of long-term care units was greater in 1965 than in
1960 in all regions under study, this pattern became more marked
between 1965 and 1970, a finding which is somewhat different from
that observed with respect to general care beds.

TABLE 9. 2

Number of Long-Term Care Units, by Size of Unit, 1960-70

Long-Term Care Units	1960		1965		1970	
	No.	Percent of Total	No.	Percent of Total	No.	Percent of Total
Under 25 beds	171	35	105	23	56	13
Under 50 beds	328	67	269	58	164	39

Source: Compiled by the author.

IMPLICATIONS OF OBSERVED DIFFERENCES

Perhaps the most noteworthy and practically significant results in this study concern changes in the number of general care beds. It will be recalled that the 1965 Governor's Committee had found evidence of a surplus of general care beds in many areas of the state. On the other hand, the committee reported an inadequate number of nursing home beds available to the population. In view of those findings, translated into statutory intent and legal mandate, a review of relevant data will be made.

In Chapter 5, it was found that a nonsignificant increase in the mean number of general care beds (132) occurred between 1960 and 1965 in all study counties. However, between 1965 and 1970 an increase of 103 beds occurred. This change proved to be statistically significant. This apparently conflicting finding can be attributed to the smaller standard error during the 1965-70 interval than the one during 1960-65. In other words, the variability in general care beds among the 25 counties was less between 1965 and 1970 than it was between 1960 and 1965. When the counties were grouped by population size, this effect occurred only in the large counties. For example, in the eight most populous counties, the mean increase during 1960 to 1965 was 358 beds (standard error, 253), while the mean increase between 1965 and 1970 was only 217 beds (standard error, 76). These results indicate that greater standardization in bed growth variability existed after 1965, a noteworthy effect, perhaps attributable to the 1965 law.

The difference in the mean number of additional beds in the less populated counties increased 96 percent (that is, from 25 beds between 1960 and 1965 to 49 during the 1965-70 interval). In both time periods the change was statistically significant. More important, the standard error showed a reverse trend to that observed in the large counties, increasing from 12 to 18 beds in the two segments of the total study period, a somewhat unexpected finding.

An interesting contrast can be found in the Rochester region. There, the differences in the number of general care beds between 1960 and 1965 and those between 1965 and 1970 were nonsignificant (in each time period, p > .10). The changes observed in the Rochester region with respect to the number of long-term care facilities were the same, that is, nonsignificant. Rochester was the only area characterized by nonsignificant differences in the mean increase in both general care and long-term care facilities during the entire study period.*

---

*The following explanation has been offered by several observers. Historically, the Rochester hospital planning council, which was established in the 1930s, held tight controls over all capital construction

New York City showed results similar to those observed in Rochester with respect to general care beds, but the variability in the growth pattern was greater between 1960 and 1965 than it was between 1965 and 1970.

These findings indicate that important changes occurred in the overall pattern of growth of general care beds in the 25 study counties. The overall average difference in general care beds was smaller after 1965 than before, and the range in the size of bed capacity was narrower. Thus less variability occurred after the law came into effect.

GROWTH PATTERNS AND ESTIMATED NEED FOR GENERAL CARE BEDS

Generally, the correlation between the growth pattern for general care beds and the estimated percent of need met for such beds was "better" before than after the introduction of the regulatory program. In the 17 small counties, the simple correlation coefficients were slightly higher, however, after the law than before.

From these findings it may be inferred that the counties' hospitals were more responsive to community need for general care beds before the law than afterwards. Large counties showed this tendency more strikingly. These findings could be explained by a changing set of medical care socioeconomic conditions that fostered the passage of the 1965 law. That is, a set of social and political forces that were simultaneously associated with a new set of hospital bed-size need standards (unlegislated) helped create the planning and legislative climate ultimately yielding the Metcalf-McCloskey Act.

On the other hand, the correlation between new general care beds occurring in the five-year intervals compared to nonconforming beds existing at the beginning of the interval was decidedly more positive after 1965. Statistically this meant that new beds increased in counties with existing numbers of nonfire-resistive structures, and that this association was stronger after implementation than before.* One could

_____

funds for new facilities and expansion projects. The control of the purse strings, in this case, provided decision-makers on the council with a powerful tool to prevent new construction not thought to be needed. That was the case before, as well as after, certificate of need legislation.

*It should be noted that 1960 data were used for this estimate of nonconforming beds for the first part of the analysis, while 1965 estimates were used for the second time period in order to show the relationship between change in general care beds and nonconformance as it existed at the beginning of each segment of the study period.

infer, therefore, that the quality of total general care beds improved
after 1965, a noteworthy change regardless of its cause.

The population variables exhibited varying relationships to change
in general care beds during the study periods. Changes in population
size were more positively associated with an increase in bed number
in all the study counties, and in large counties, during the period 1960-
65 than for the period 1965-70. However, the opposite was true for
the smaller counties and three of the planning regions. Where there
was static or decreasing population size, the purpose of the law
seemed somewhat thwarted. The explanation for this observation is
undoubtedly complex and involves inferences requiring social and
political data beyond the scope of this study.

On the other hand, size of population seemed to be more closely
associated with change in the number of general care beds after the
program's implementation than before, except in the northern metropolitan and Long Island regions. This suggests that except for the
northern metropolitan and Long Island regions, changes in the number
of general care beds were more closely linked to population size after
1965 than before.

While changes in bed capacity were positively associated with
population growth in the period 1960 to 1965, in the larger counties the
strength of that association weakened between 1965 and 1970. From
this one could infer that factors other than population growth tended to
become more important after 1965. Such changes that exceeded the
planner's stated needs in that time period may reflect softness in
administration of the law or a change in the responsiveness of planners
to conditions not included in the need allotment formulae. An example
may be the apparent increased growth and use of specialized facilities
and services centralized in the large teaching centers located in urban
centers.

Many nonresidents seem to seek their specialized care in the
large urban academic medical centers, a pattern documented by Blue
Cross/Blue Shield of Greater New York (Associated Hospital Service).
This should be taken into account as need estimates are developed in
the future for the regions of New York State. (The Task Force on General and Specialty Hospital Care of the New York State Health Planning
Commission has incorporated the concepts of primary, secondary, and
tertiary care in developing the Plan for New York State, 1974-75.)

GROWTH PATTERNS AND ESTIMATED NEED
FOR LONG-TERM CARE BEDS

An examination of the simple correlation coefficients between
change in the number of long-term care beds and a set of selected

independent variables showed that there were only slight differences between the two time periods.

For example, there seems to have been little consistency in the associations between changes in the number of long-term beds and the estimated percent of need met for such beds.

The correlation coefficients between the long-term bed increase and nonconforming beds showed that the correlation for all study counties was slightly higher after implementation than before. There was a substantial change in the correlation in the large counties after 1965, but the direction was negative, opposite that expected. (This may represent a statistical artifact on this study design which was aimed at a 95 percent confidence interval.)

No change was apparent in the smaller counties, but there was a positive change in the northern metropolitan and Long Island regions. Rochester showed a high correlation for both periods. (See note on pages 109-10 for a possible explanation.)

The simple correlations between change in the number of long-term care beds and the four independent population variables generally shifted in the positive direction during the second segment of the study period, 1965 to 1970. The most sizable drift in correlations occurred between long-term care beds and population size 65 years and older, confirming the hypothesis that in the postlaw period, change in the number of long-term care beds was more sensitive to the size of the 65 and older population group.

For the larger counties, change in population size seemed a weaker indicator of changes in long-term care beds for 1965 to 1970 than for 1960 to 1965. These findings suggest that where there are large population concentrations, such as in the large counties in this study, the change in population for a comparatively small group like those 65 and over is a more sensitive indicator than change in total population size.

In summary, one can conclude that the law seemed to have an intended effect on long-term care bed construction in the study counties. The effect was most marked in counties with large population concentrations, and the best indicator of that effect was the change in the 65 and over population after the law's passage.

RESULTS OF THE MULTIPLE REGRESSION ANALYSIS

The results of the multiple regression analysis indicated that, when all the independent variables were taken into account, there were varying effects before and after introduction of the certificate of need program. These were observed with respect to general care as well as long-term care beds.

During the 1960-65 interval, the variance in the growth of general care beds was significantly associated with population size, population

65 and over, change in population 65 and over, the number of nonconforming general care beds, median family income, and house staff.
Population size, change in population size, and house staff were positively associated with change in the number of general care beds, while
the number of nonconforming general care beds, population 65 and over,
and median family income showed a negative association to bed growth.
Between 1965 and 1960, number of physicians, population 65 and over,
and change in population size were the best predictors.

These findings imply that before 1965, increases in the number of
general care beds in the study counties occurred generally where there
was a large population and there was an increase in population size.
The negative correlation between bed expansion and the number of nonconforming beds seems to imply, on the other hand, that before 1965,
the expansion of facilities was not associated with reduction of the
problem of nonconformance. Moreover, the negative association
between increased general care beds and population 65 and over seems
to imply that before the law, the growth of facilities occurred in areas
with a small 65 and over population size. After implementation, that
association shifted from negative to positive and the difference was
statistically significant. The same was true with respect to nonconforming general care beds

When all the independent variables were taken into account the
analysis showed that changes in long-term care beds, before 1965,
were significantly associated with number of physicians, change in
population 65 and over, nonconforming long-term care beds, median
family income, house staff, and nonconforming general care beds.
After introduction of the certificate of need program, physicians,
change in population 65 and over, median family income, and house
staff were the best predictors. That association changed from negative
before 1965 to positive after in the case of the change in population
65 and over as well as for house staff. The same was true for nonconforming long-term care beds, and the change between the 1960-65
time interval and the 1965 70 period was statistically significant. The
association between change in long-term care beds and number of
physicians changed from positive to negative, while median family
income remained positively associated with long-term care bed growth
for both the before and after periods.

These findings suggest that changes in the 65 and over population
were more positively associated with changes in longterm care facilities
after implementation of the program than before, an observation first
made on the basis of zero-order correlations, and confirmed here by
multiple regression. The effect of Medicare in the 1965-70 period,
however, confounds a favorable inference about the effect of the
certificate of need legislation. In addition, we will recall that the
Article 28A program was intended to stimulate construction of nonprofit nursing homes in underserved areas. Applications for construction funds under that program required certificate of need approval.
One can infer from these data that intended results were obtained.

CONCLUSIONS

The data in this study suggest that since 1965, coinciding with the implementation of certificate of need in New York State, changes in hospital beds and long-term care facilities have occurred in a mixed pattern. No simple summation is possible as to either the results or their interpretation.

General Care Beds

On the average, fewer general care beds had been added in the 25 study counties during the five years after implementation than during the five years before. This is especially important because of the potential for a building boom in short-term general hospitals following enactment of the Medicare legislation in 1965.[3] Not only was the average number of additional hospital beds smaller, but there was reduced variability, suggesting more uniformity in planning for such facilities.

Moreover, after 1965, increases in general care beds tended to occur mainly in counties identified at the beginning of the interval 1965-70 as having a number of nonconforming hospital beds. This relationship seemed to improve after introduction of the certificate of need program, suggesting beneficial results of the program.

The simple correlation between change in the number of general care beds and change in population size was weaker after 1965 than before in all counties, suggesting an undesired outcome. That is, general care beds appeared to be added in areas where either population change was negative or where it was relatively stable.

To some extent the negative aspects of these findings have been partially confirmed. In a study reported in 1974 by Lowell E. Bellin, Commissioner of Health of the City of New York, an excess of municipal hospital beds was identified in the Bronx, creating financial difficulties in the municipal health care system in New York City.[4]

Similar problems of overbedding were noted in other areas of New York City as well, suggesting that while the regulatory power to disapprove unnecessary beds was available, it may not have been adequately exercised.* It should be noted that all four New York City

---

*Between 1960 and 1973, the number of municipal hospital beds actually declined in the Bronx. However, the overall number of available beds in that county will exceed the number of estimated beds needed by 1978 by over 330, according to New York State Department of Health figures (Municipal Hospital Bed Needs in The Bronx: A Staff

counties included among the large study counties experienced small
population changes during the study period. In the case of Kings and
New York counties, an actual outmigration of population occurred. *

Because of the size and relative population size stability in these
large counties of New York City, the apparent negative effect in the
Bronx, Kings, Queens, and New York county seem to reflect the problem identified by Bellin.

In contrast to these findings, the association between increased
beds and change in population size was positive and stronger after
1965 than before in the 17 smaller counties, as well as in the Rochester,
Long Island and northern metropolitan regions. This outcome occurred
in the expected direction. One can infer that after 1965, population
growth became a better predictor of change in general care beds in
these counties and regions than before.

On the other hand, association between changes in the number of
general care beds and estimated need for such facilities in the counties
under study did not occur as expected. Whereas a negative correlation
was anticipated (that is, fewer beds added where percent of need met
was high and vice versa), the opposite was found.

From the data presented above, one can infer that after 1965,
coinciding with the introduction of the certificate of need program,
there were changes in hospital bed construction that occurred in the
opposite direction intended by the law, reversing earlier trends which
were in the intended direction. In almost each instance, the correlation
was better (more negative) before the program was implemented than
after.

These findings are difficult to explain but may be attributable to
inadequate preparation of need estimates, or to a disregard of estimates
by planning councils during the review process. Or they may reflect a
less than vigorous approach to carrying out the mandate of the law.
Sorting out the probable cause extends beyond the scope of this research,
but it points out the need for additional research into these questions.

It may be concluded from these findings that there are areas in
need of change in the application or even perhaps in the certificate of
need legislation itself. Though retarding the construction of unneeded
hospital beds has seemingly been accomplished, the inference can be
drawn that facilities may have been located in places where their need
was low, and vice versa, at least by the data criteria used in this study.

Position Paper. Appendix F prepared by Marietta Meyer, New York
City Health and Hospitals Corporation, October 30, 1974).

*Richmond was not included among the largest counties because
of the population size (under 300, 000 in 1970) and because of the
rapid growth in population size between 1960 and 1970 (33. 1 percent),
thereby distinguishing Richmond from the other four counties of New
York City.

Long-Term Care Beds

The results were somewhat different with respect to long-term care beds. During the 1960-65 time interval, few counties under study appeared to have a sufficient number of suitable long-term care beds to meet the accelerating demand. (It will be recalled that in 1960 the data indicated that nearly half of the 25 counties did not have suitable facilities, and in three of the four study regions, 65 percent or more of the available beds were in nonfire-resistive structures.)

The increase in the number of long-term care beds was three times greater after introduction of the certificate of need program than before (35 percent between 1965 and 1970 as opposed to 11 percent between 1960 and 1965). Moreover, the reduction in the number of nonconforming long-term care beds was far more dramatic after implementation than before.

These results are probably attributable to the effect of the law as well as to the other recommendations of the Folsom Committee and the enactment of Medicare. The Folsom Committee, in its report to the governor, had identified the need for additional conforming long-term care facilities. Passage of the Medicare legislation in 1965 only served to accentuate these needs. As a result, Article 28 had been amended almost immediately after its enactment to encourage construction of needed nonprofit nursing homes throughout the state. The outcomes seem to indicate that some of the program's objectives have been achieved. By 1970, there were new conforming nursing home and chronic care beds available to the population most in need of them. Moreover, expansion seemed to correlate better, generally, with change in population 65 and over after implementation than before.

An interesting local development in New York City is worth mentioning here. Since 1965, much of the new nursing home construction occurred in one area, namely, the Rockaways. The approval of these projects must have seemed reasonable when made, but there have been recent repercussions as vocal community groups have increasingly protested the concentration of such facilities. As a consequence, the New York City Planning Commission amended the city charter requiring approval by local community boards before nursing homes may be constructed or expanded in their neighborhoods.

DIRECTIONS FOR FUTURE RESEARCH

This study examined the impact of regulating health facility expansion, through certification of need, on health planning outcomes. While the study allowed an exploration of positive benefits, as well as unexpected outcomes, which were associated with and may be attributed to the introduction of this regulatory program, the study was not designed to cover other kinds of analyses which would be useful in evaluating the program.

A most intriguing question which remains unanswered, for example, is what might have been if New York State had not enacted this kind of legislative program. While it would probably be difficult to find states with similar characteristics to those of New York State but which had not enacted certificate of need laws during the study period, it might be useful to select counties or planning regions of New York State for comparison with similar counties and regions in states with no certificate of need program during the study period in order to observe the effect of national health programs and policies, such as Medicare, Comprehensive Health Planning, and Regional Medical Programs, on outcomes as defined in this study.

Another fruitful line of inquiry might be an economic analysis of the certificate of need program in relation to hospital costs. Those who advocated the legislation had made certain assumptions about controlling hospital expansion and the impact such controls might have on costs. In view of the findings presented here, that the overall expansion of general care beds did slow down after introduction of the program, it might be useful to determine what the relationship has been between hospital expansionism and hospital costs.

A careful exploration of the planning process, as carried out during the study period, might illuminate how decisions were made and by whom, which interest groups were most deeply involved, and which groups were underrepresented. Questions might be raised regarding how priorities were established, what guidelines were used, under what circumstances there were disagreements between local planning councils and state councils, and whether political influence was used to obtain approval of projects which were not necessarily in the public interest.

Finally, it would be important to determine what impact the certificate of need program has had on institutional planning, if any— whether there were shifts in the types of applications submitted by hospitals and other institutions under the Article 28 purview. Such a study would naturally have to take into account changes in the economy and in reimbursement policies as well as utilization patterns which might have accounted for differences in planning activities observed at the institutional level.

EPILOGUE

In June 1974, three major health planning bills, Regional Medical Programs (RMP), Comprehensive Health Planning (CHP), and the Hill-Burton Program, were due to expire. Prior to that date, a number of alternative bills had been introduced in both the Senate and House of Representatives, most of them incorporating the certificate of need approach to controlling hospital beds. In the absence of a consensus, the Congress simply extended the existing authorities for one year.

During the weeks and months that followed, various congressional committees heard testimony on proposals for solving the nation's health planning problems for the late 1970s and beyond.

On January 4, 1975, Pub. L. 93--641, the National Planning and Resources Development Act, became law. In essence, the act combines RMP, CHP, and Hill-Burton functions. Planning and development activities are to be administered by regional health systems agencies serving between half a million and three million people. These agencies will be charged with planning responsibilities for their designated areas and will be authorized to recommend approval or disapproval of new beds or changes in existing services or facilities.

The regulatory authority for final approval or disapproval of proposed changes in facilities and services is vested in a state agency to be designated by the governor and is based on certification of need.

In future studies of the effectiveness of this landmark legislation—in which New York's experiment has become national public policy—it is hoped that the methodology and findings presented in this study will provide some useful approaches to the complex problem of analyzing and evaluating the program's impact.

NOTES

1. William Levy, The Article 28 Story (unpublished mimeograph), 1972, p. 2.

2. Ibid.

3. See, for example, a series of articles by Victor Cohn, "Unplanned Hospitals: An Uncontrolled Boom in the Washington, D. C. Area," a six-part series in the Washington Post (August-September, 1974).

4. New York City Department of Health, Office of Program Analysis and Planning, Municipal Hospital Beds in the Borough of the Bronx: Projected Demand and Costs, mimeographed (September 18, 1974).

DESCRIPTION OF ALL DEPENDENT AND INDEPENDENT VARIABLES

All variables were regressed for each segment of the study period (1960-65 and 1965-70).

Y_1 = Change in the number of general care beds[a]

Y_2 = Change in the number of long-term care beds[a]

X_1 = Population size[b]

X_2 = Change in population size[c]

X_3 = Population 65 years of age and over[b]

X_4 = Change in population 65 years of age and over[c]

X_5 = Number of nonconforming general care beds[d]

X_6 = Number of nonconforming long-term care beds[d]

X_7 = Percent of need met—general care beds[e]

X_8 = Percent of need met—long-term care beds[e]

X_9 = Number of nonfederal physicians

X_{10} = Number of house staff

X_{11} = Median family income

---

[a]Computed for each segment of the study period from data in New York State Plans for Construction of Hospital and Related Facilities.

[b]Based on 1960 and 1970 census data.

[c]Computed from 1960 and 1970 census data.

[d]Includes only those classified as nonfire-resistive.

[e]Based on data from New York State Plan for Construction of Hospital and Related Facilities (1960 and 1965).

American Hospital Association. Guidelines for Implementation of Certification of Need for Health Care Facilities and Services. Chicago, Illinois: 1972.

American Medical Association. Directory of Approved Internships and Residencies. Chicago, Illinois, 1967-68, 1971-72.

_____. Distribution of Physicians in the United States by State, Region, District and County. Chicago, Illinois, 1959, 1966.

Binch, Frank. "Tomorrow's Hospital Bed Population." Hospital Forum, May, 1974.

Bridgman, R. F., and Roemer, M. I. Hospital Legislation and Hospital Systems, Public Health Papers No. 50, World Health Organization, 1973.

Brown, Douglas R. "The Areawide Hospital Planning Process," Doctoral dissertation, Cornell University, Ithaca, New York, 1971.

California Hospital Association, Policy Statement on Governmental Regulation. August, 1974.

Cavanaugh, James H. "Areawide Planning for Hospitals and Related Health Facilities," Ph.D. dissertation, University of Iowa, 1964.

Cohen, Harris. "Regulating Health Care Facilities: The Certificate of Need Process Re-Examined," Inquiry 10 (September, 1973).

Cohn, Victor. "Unplanned Hospitals: An Uncontrolled Boom in the Washington, D.C. Area." A six-part series from the Washington Post, August-September, 1973.

Comptroller General of the United States. Report to the Congress, "Study of Health Facilities Construction Costs." Washington, D.C.: Joint Committee Print, 92nd Congress, 2nd Session, U.S. Government Printing Office, 1972.

Draper, N. R., and Smith, H. Applied Regression Analysis. New York, London, Sydney: John Wiley and Sons, Inc., 1966.

Elsasser, Peter J., and Galinski, Thomas P. "Certificate of Need, Status of State Legislation," Hospitals 45 (December 16, 1971).

Epstein, Richard L. "Relevance of the Public Utility Concept to the Health Care Industry, " The Hospital Forum, September, 1972.

Fry, Hilary G. The Operation of State Hospital Planning and Licensing Programs. Chicago, Illinois: American Hospital Association, 1965.

Glaude, Arthur. "An Analysis of Article 28-B, Dormitory Authority and Hill-Burton Guaranteed Loan with Interest Subsidy Capital Financing Programs for Hospitals." Hospital Association of New York State, 1973.

Havighurst, Clark C. "Public Utility Regulation for Hospitals: The Relevance of Experience in Other Regulated Industries, " Reprint No. 17. Washington, D. C.: American Enterprise Institute for Public Policy Research, 1974.

_____. "Regulation of Health Facilities and Services by Certificate of Need. " Virginia Law Review 59 (October, 1973).

_____, ed. Regulating Health Facilities Construction. Proceedings of a Conference on Health Planning, Certificates of Need, and Market Entry, Washington, D.C.: American Enterprise Institute for Public Policy Research, 1973.

Helms, Robert B. Natural Gas Regulation: An Evaluation of FPC Price Controls. Washington, D. C.: American Enterprise Institute for Public Policy Research, 1974.

Ingbar, Mary Lee. "Hospital Costs and Efficiency, A Report to the California Hospital Commission on Its Prospects and Problems. " San Francisco, California: Health Policy Program and Division of Ambulatory and Community Medicine, School of Medicine, University of California, 1973.

Katz, Leonard William. "An Evaluation of the State of Connecticut Health and Educational Authority's Impact on the Provision of Non-governmental Health Facilities." Doctoral dissertation, The George Washington University, Washington, D. C., 1972.

Klarman, Herbert E. "Some Technical Problems in Areawide Planning for Hospital Care. " Journal of Chronic Diseases 17, 1964.

Lave, Judith R., and Lave, Lester B. The Hospital Construction Act: An Evaluation of the Hill-Burton Program, 1948-1973. Washington, D. C.: American Enterprise Institute for Public Policy Research, 1974.

Leavy, William. "The Article 28 Story: New York State's National Leadership in Health Facility Planning." Mimeographed, 1972.

Lewinski-Corwin, E. L. The Hospital Situation in Greater New York. New York Academy of Medicine, Putnam's, 1924.

McNerney, Walter J., and Riedel, Donald C. Regionalization and Rural Health Care. Research Series Number 2, Ann Arbor, Michigan: University of Michigan, Bureau of Hospital Administration, 1962.

May, Joel J. Health Planning: Its Past and Potential, Health Administration Perspectives. Chicago, Illinois: University of Chicago, Center for Health Administration Studies, 1967.

Medical Care for the American People, The Final Report of the Committee on the Costs of Medical Care, Reprinted by the Department of Health, Education, and Welfare, 1970.

Morris, Robert. "The City of the Future and Planning for Health," American Journal of Public Health 58 (January, 1968).

Mott, Basil. "The Myth of Planning Without Politics." American Journal of Public Health 59 (May, 1969).

National Advisory Commission of Health Facilities. A Report to the President, 1968. Washington, D.C.: U.S. Government Printing Office, 1968.

Navarro, Vincente. Methodology in Regionalization and Health Planning. Baltimore, Department of Medical Care and Hospitals, The Johns Hopkins University School of Hygiene, Mimeographed, 1967.

New York Academy of Medicine. "Closing the Gaps in the Availability and Accessibility of Health Services." Bulletin of the New York Academy of Medicine, December, 1965.

New York City Commission on the Delivery of Personal Health Services. Comprehensive Community Health Services for New York City: A Report. New York: Office of the Mayor, 1968.

New York City Planning Commission. Amendments of the Zoning Resolution Pursuant to Section 200 of the New York City Charter, Calendar Numbers 1 and 2. January 7, 1974.

New York City Department of Health, Office of Program Analysis and Planning. "Municipal Hospital Beds in the Borough of the Bronx: Projected Demand and Costs." September, 1974.

New York City Health and Hospital Corporation. "Municipal Hospital
    Bed Needs in the Bronx: A Staff Position Paper." October, 1974.

New York State Department of Health, New York State Plan for Health
    Facility Development. 1970-71.

_____. Bureau of Facility Planning, "Determination of Need and
    Project Review," Policy and Procedures Manual, n. d.

_____. Division of Hospital Review and Planning, New York State
    Plan for Construction of Hospitals and Related Facilities. 1965-66.

New York State Joint Hospital Survey and Planning Commission. New
    York State Plan for Construction of Hospitals and Related Facilities.
    1959-1960.

Noll, Roger G. "The Consequences of Public Utility Regulation of
    Hospitals." Mimeographed.

Palmiere, Darwin; Freeborn, Donald K.; Lewis, Joann; Hughes, Pamela.
    Health Facilities Planning Council Evaluation Project Reports One
    Through Five. Health Services and Mental Health Administration,
    1971.

"Report of the Governor's Committee on Hospital Costs," final report.
    Albany, 1965.

"Report of the Governor's Steering Committee on Social Problems on
    Health and Hospital Services and Costs." State of New York,
    1971.

"Report of the Joint Legislative Committee on Health Insurance Plans."
    New York Legislative Documents, No. 39, 1964.

"Report to the Chairman of the New York City Planning Commission."
    Medical Facility Expansion Task Force, New York City Department
    of City Planning, June, 1974.

Roemer, Milton I. "Bed Supply and Hospital Untilization: A Natural
    Experiment." Hospitals 35 (November, 1961).

Rogatz, Peter. "Ambulatory Care: Digging Out From Under the Bricks
    and Mortar." Paper presented to the American Health Congress,
    August 20, 1973.

_____. "Let's Get Rid of Those Surplus Hospital Beds." Prism,
    October, 1974.

Rosenthal, Gerald. The Demand for General Hospital Facilities. Chicago, Illinois: American Hospital Association, 1964.

Sattler, Frederic L., and Bennett, Max D. "A Statistical Profile of Short-Term Hospitals in the United States as of 1973." Minneapolis, Minnesota: Interstudy, January, 1975.

Selected Papers on Health Planning: Its Purpose, Evaluating Outcomes, Health Administration Perspectives, No. A8, Chicago, Illinois: University of Chicago, 1969.

Selltiz, Claire; Jahoda, Marie; Deutsch, Morton; and Cook, Stuart W. Research Methods in Social Relations. New York: Holt, Rinehart and Winston, 1959.

Somers, Anne R. "Medicare—Way to Make Planning Effective." Modern Hospital 108 (June, 1967).

_____. "Some Basic Determinants of Medical Care and Health Policy: An Overview of Trends and Issues." Milbank Memorial Fund Quarterly 46 (January, 1968), pt. 2.

_____. Hospital Regulation: The Dilemma of Public Policy. Princeton, N.J.: Industrial Relations Section, Princeton University, 1969.

_____. "State Regulation of Hospitals and Health Care: The New Jersey Story." Blue Cross Reports, Research Series 11, July, 1973.

Somers, Herman Miles, and Somers, Anne Ramsay. Doctors, Patients, and Health Insurance. Washington, D.C.: The Brookings Institution, 1961.

_____. Medicare and the Hospitals, Washington, D.C.: The Brookings Institution, 1967.

Thomas, William C., Jr. Nursing Homes and Public Policy: Drift and Reunion in New York State. Ithaca, New York: Cornell University Press, 1969.

Treolar, Alan E., and Chill, Don. Patient Care Facilities: Construction Needs and Hill-Burton Accomplishments. Chicago, Illinois: American Hospital Association, 1961.

Trussell, Ray E., and others. Status of Implementation of the Recommendations of the Governor's Committee on Hospital Costs, Two Years of Experience, 1965-67. New York: Columbia University, 1967.

Trussell, Ray E.; Ehrlich, June; and Morehead, Mildred A. The
    Quantity, Quality, and Costs of Medical Care Secured by a Sample
    of Teamster Families in the New York Area. New York: Columbia
    University School of Public Health and Administrative Medicine,
    1960.

U. S. Bureau of the Census. County and City Data Book. 1967-72.

U. S. Bureau of the Census, Census of Population: 1970, General
    Population Characteristics Final Report PC (1)-B34. New York,
    1972.

U. S. Department of Health, Education and Welfare. "The Certificate
    of Need Experience: An Early Assessment." Bureau of Health
    Services Research, April, 1974.

Wennberg, John, and Gittlesohn, Alan. "Small Area Variations in
    Health Care Delivery." Science 182 (December 14, 1973).

Zwick, Daniel, and Hersch, Jay. "State Advisory Boards: What They
    Do Now, What They May Do Tomorrow." Modern Hospital, May,
    1973.

ELEANORE ROTHENBERG, Executive Director of the New York County
Health Services Review Organization (NYCHSRO), the Professional
Standards Review Organization (PSRO) for New York County, is an
expert in health policy, planning, and administration. Before joining
NYCHSRO, Dr. Rothenberg served first as an associate in health
services research and planning, then was associate director of policy
analysis at New York University Medical Center. She has been a
consultant in the Department of Health, Education, and Welfare on
alcoholism and alcohol abuse, and since 1974 has served as a member
of the committee on the use of human subjects in research for the New
York City Department of Health.

Dr. Rothenberg was a consultant to the Governor's Special Advisory
Committee on Medical Malpractice. Her recommendations and staff
paper were included in the panel's final report to the governor and
legislature of New York State.

While at New York University Medical Center, Dr. Rothenberg
coordinated the hospital administration residency and acted as preceptor
in a number of experimental study programs. She has been a frequent
guest lecturer on modern management of health delivery systems, and
in 1976 was invited to join the faculty of Columbia University School
of Public Health and Administrative Medicine.

Dr. Rothenberg received her Ph.D. from New York University
Graduate School of Arts and Sciences, writing her dissertation on the
impact of certificate of need on hospital and health facilities planning
outcomes, from which this book is derived.

ACCOUNTABILITY IN HEALTH FACILITIES
Harry I. Greenfield

AMERICAN HEALTH: Professional Privilege
vs. Public Need
Tom Levin

CHANGING THE MEDICAL CARE SYSTEM: A
Controlled Experiment in Comprehensive Care
Leon S. Robertson, John Kosa,
Margaret C. Heagarty, Robert J.
Haggerty, and Joel J. Alpert

THE DESIGN OF A HEALTH MAINTENANCE
ORGANIZATION: A Handbook for Practitioners
Allan Easton

HOSPITAL EFFICIENCY AND PUBLIC POLICY
Harry I. Greenfield

THE POLITICS OF HEALTH CARE: Nine Case
Studies of Innovative Planning in New York City
edited by Herbert Harvey Hyman